Judge Woody:

History and Humor in the Old West

Compilation and Commentary

By

Traci L. Rasmusson D.C.

Porte de L'Enfer Publishing - Missoula, MT

Contents

Preface

This book was the result of hours of research I engaged in during the pandemic of 2020. I started looking through old newspapers while putting together my coffee table book *Finding Old Missoula*. In the course of perusing newspapers, I kept stumbling across stories told by and about Judge Frank Woody, one of Missoula, Montana's founding fathers. I was soon drawn in by his dry humor and his vivid recollections of the old west. I couldn't believe no one had done a compilation of his stories. I decided to remedy this error once I was finished writing *Finding Old Missoula*.

The result of my research ends up not only teaching us more about the early history of settlers in the old west but also yields a fairly in-depth biography of Judge Woody's life. The reader must be cautioned that Mr. Woody (and Mr. Stone) sometimes used words and phrases that may be considered offensive to Indigenous Americans and Black Americans. His use of these words reflects the ignorance and a certain arrogance white people had in the United States in the 1800's (and later) towards non-whites. After much soul searching, I have decided to keep them in this book. Please understand that I do not condone using these words or phrases or take them lightly. After reading newspaper articles throughout Judge Woody's life, I can tell you that he had a reputation for fairness and called people "friend" who were not white or Christian. He also acknowledged the great wrong done to the Native Tribes of western Montana by the United States Government in an article written in his old age.

You will note that some of the pieces were written by him as essays for journals and the newspaper and some were written about him as newspaper articles. The pieces that were written about him were most likely done by Arthur L. Stone, noted Montana journalist who worked at the Anaconda

Standard then moved to the Daily Missoulian. Mr. Stone also started the Journalism School at the University of Montana. He and Judge Woody were good friends and he seemed to enjoy poking fun at the Judge in print. When I could corroborate for certain that he had written an article, I gave him credit.

Another note, the Judge's stories often repeat themselves…so in some instances in this compilation, you will read the same story again. Usually, the duplicate will include information not shared in a prior story or it is part of another story not shared previously.

Enjoy!

Traci Rasmusson D.C.
January 2, 2021

Introduction

Frank H. Woody was born in 1833 in Chatham, North Carolina. His father was a Quaker, and his mother was descended from American revolutionaries. After a rudimentary early education, he spent one year at Guilford College (a Quaker school). Once he graduated from Guilford, he spent several years teaching in public schools before making the decision to seek his fortune out west. In 1855 he traveled to Salt Lake City and eventually signed on to drive a team of oxen and a wagon to present day Ravalli and Missoula counties. This move began his residence in western Montana which lasted until his death in 1916.

Woody clerked in the Trading Post started by Frank Worden and Captain Christopher Higgins in Hellgate Ronde, the first white settlement in the Missoula Valley. He took on many roles in Hellgate then in Missoula. He was the Postmaster, County Clerk and Recorder then Probate Judge. He was also the deputy clerk for the Second Judicial District. Finding that he had an affinity for the law, Woody studied the law and was admitted to the bar in 1877. Later on, he became Missoula's first mayor then Judge of the Fourth District. (Hence the name "Judge Woody".)

Judge Woody married Elizabeth Countryman in 1871. They had eight children, unfortunately only three survived to adulthood. Mrs. Woody suffered from poor health for most of their marriage possibly due to childhood injuries suffered after she fell into a campfire.

The Judge's dry humor and self-deprecating manner made him a well-loved character in Missoula and western Montana. When he died in 1916, his loss was keenly felt all over the state.

Judge F.H. Woody.

Judge Woody in the 1880's

(From the Archival Photos from the University of Montana #76.11

How an Early Pioneer Came to Montana and the Privations Encountered on the Journey

BY FRANK H. WOODY, OF MISSOULA, MONTANA

———————

I have often been urged to write up a series of articles concerning matters which transpired in the early days of Montana, and of which I had a personal knowledge, but up to the present time have, for various reasons, neglected to do so. Recently I have been urged by some old-time friends and pioneers to write an article to be published in Volume VII of the Contributions to the Historical Society, and have reluctantly consented to do so, giving an account of my journey from the Missouri river, to what is now the State of Montana, and some account of the many difficulties met with in the journey.

In 1854 Congress passed the Kansas-Nebraska Act, organizing the territories of Kansas and Nebraska, and in the spring of 1855, there was a wonderful emigration to these new territories, and especially to Kansas. In the month of April of that year I joined the rush for Kansas and arrived at Leavenworth City about the 19th of April, 1855 with about $35.00 in my pocket. Leavenworth City then contained seven or eight buildings, all built of green cottonwood boards.

On my way up the river on the steamboat I made the acquaintance of three or four young fellows of about my own age, and all of them of my limited means. We kept together, looking to see what we could do, and soon our money was all gone, and something had to be done. During this time one of our number, a young man from Memphis, Tennessee, died with the cholera and things began to look serious for us.

We heard that the U.S. Quartermaster at Fort Leavenworth wanted men to drive mule teams from Fort Leavenworth up to some fort on the Missouri river, and we thought we would like the job, though none of us had ever driven a mule team. We went up to see the quartermaster and he directed us to go down to the government corrals, about three miles below the city, and report to the man in charge, and that he would employ us. We went down, but before reporting to the man in charge, we concluded to look into the nature of the employment. We stayed there a few hours and saw them breaking in teams of big, wild mules, and concluded we did not want any of that kind of work, so we did not ask for a job, but returned to the city.

When we returned to Leavenworth, we there found a Mormon named John Waddell, who was intending to outfit a large train of wagons to haul merchandise to Salt Lake City. He had bought a portion of his cattle and was still after the others. We hired to him at twenty-five dollars a month and were put to herding cattle on foot just back of Leavenworth City, and did herd them, day and night, on foot, up to the latter part of May. He had established a camp back of what was then Leavenworth, and about a mile from the river, where our tents were then located. At that time there were but three stores in Salt Lake: Livingston & Kincaid, Gilbert & Gerrish and Hooper & Williams: all of them, at that time, about out of goods. Waddell had a contract to haul goods from the Missouri river to Salt Lake City for Livingston & Kincaid.

About the latter part of May we commenced getting up our cattle and branding them, which took several days. We then proceeded to get them up and yoke them, and in order to do so, most of the cattle had to be lassoed and snubbed to a post, the majority of them being wild cattle, and a majority of the hired men who had been hired as teamsters, were Mormon emigrants. Waddell had, however, a few experienced teamsters, and several of us green Americans, who knew nothing about ox teams. About the last of May it commenced raining and it rained for about eight or ten days, until the ground was perfectly miry. Along in the early days of June we had got the wagons loaded and were preparing to start on our journey. The morning on which we were to start the order was given to the teamsters to yoke up their teams. A few of the old teamsters, knowing the gentle cattle, selected good teams, leaving the others for the Mormons and the green Americans to hitch up. The wagon-master finally interfered and made these experienced teamsters turn some of their gentle cattle over to the other teamsters and take, in their place, some of the wild, unbroken cattle. We had forty-six wagons in our train, running from two to six-yoke to a wagon. Not one of these Englishmen and very few of the green Americans had ever driven an ox and knew nothing about oxen or ox-teams. We had three wagon-masters, the head man, Dan Patterson, was a Cherokee breed, who had been across the plains a number of times and was an experienced man, and it turned out that Livingston & Kincaid, for whom Waddell was freighting, had promised Patterson a considerable bonus if he would get that train of merchandise in Salt Lake City in advance of the other trains. His first assistant was a man named Perry Dillon, the second assistant was a young fellow named Simpson. Dillon had been across the plains a number of times and was an experienced wagon-master, but both he and Patterson were overbearing and brutal to the men.

We started from camp on the fifth of June, and of all the teaming that ever was seen, I presume that beat all. These Mormons and the green Americans knowing nothing about the work, did not know how to handle their teams or to make them pull. The result was, we were from early morning until dark in making three miles to Salt Creek. I remember very well the team I was driving was a four-yoke team. The pair of leaders was old, and would not keep out of the way of the others. The wheelers were fairly good, while the two yoked in the middle were wild. In those days wagons had no brakes on them, but lock chains were used altogether. We had to pass through a lane in the government farm at Fort Leavenworth, and in doing so had to pass down a long incline, not very steep, I could not make my wheelers hold the wagon back, and when I locked it, I could not make them pull it, so, in order to get on, I unlocked it and they ran into the government fence, and tore down about ten rods of it, when the wagon-master came back and pulled me out. After two or three days, we had things in better working order, and got along fairly well. We arrived at the Little Blue River, where a little town had been started, called Marysville, and this was the last of civilization that we saw, except old Fort Laramie and Fort Kearney, and one trading-post, until we arrived at Salt Lake City. Patterson, in order to earn his bonus, drove us late and early, and the men were worn out. We would start early in the morning and drive till about eleven o'clock, corral our wagons, turn our cattle loose, wait until about two o'clock, then drive the cattle in, hitch up and drive till dark: then by the time we got our supper and got to bed, it was quite late, and we were called in the morning about four o'clock. The result was that in a short time the men were tired out and nearly dead for sleep.

The wagon-master and his first assistant used to abuse the Mormons fearfully. I have seen them beaten severely with ox-bows and offer no resistance whatever, but they never tried this on the Americans.

After we passed through Fort Kearney, we struck the buffalo country and for about three days travelled through a section of country where we were never out of sight of buffalo. The plains were dotted with them. Things went on in this way until we arrived at a point on the Platte river about eight miles above old Fort Laramie where we camped for that night. That afternoon rations had been issued to the various messes (there being seven in number) for one week. Each teamster was furnished with a gun, which was strapped on the outside of the wagon, the guns being known as the government Yagers, or Mississippi rifles. Each teamster had also a liberal supply of ammunition. This for protection against the Indians, as the Sioux that season were hostile and on the warpath, and the road, or a portion of it, was patrolled by government troops, and later in the season, Gen. Harney had a fight with the Sioux, at Ash Hollow, and defeated them. When we arrived at this point on the Platte river, about eight miles above Fort Laramie, we encamped for the night. In our party of young Americans was a young man, a medical graduate from Rush Medical College, Chicago, named Bates, who was acting as commissary for the train. Patterson, the head wagon-master, had a liberal supply of whiskey aboard and kept drunk a great portion of the time. After we arrived at camp that evening, he and Bates had some difficulty, and he drew his pistol upon

14

Bates, but did not shoot. That evening or that night, our crowd of young Americans and one Englishman, to the number of nine, held a consultation and concluded we would stand their abuse no longer. We would not stand being driven night and day, and decided we would leave the train. So that night, after all hands had gone to bed, we took all the mess-kit belonging to one mess, and all the rations that we could carry, with our blankets, each man being loaded with about 150 pounds, and silently stole away from the camp, climbing a bluff two or three hundred feet high, which over looked the camp, deposited our plunder, put out a guard, laid down and went to sleep.

Early next morning it was discovered that a part of the teamsters were missing and we were discovered on top of this bluff. Patterson sent two or three Mexicans he had to us for the purpose of bringing us into camp and compelling us to go on. We piled up our flour sacks and blankets and got behind them. We then told the Mexicans to go back, if not, we would fire on them. They saw we were determined, and soon returned to camp---nine teamsters gone. They commenced to chain up their lighter wagons to the heavier, and finally, about ten o'clock, proceeded. After they were well out of the way, each man gathered up his load and we all went down to the Platte river, went into camp, put out a guard and went to sleep. We had the intention, when we hired to Waddell at Leavenworth, of driving the teams to Salt Lake, and then, with the money that was coming to us, club together, buy a few pack animals, and go to California. Up to this time we had been paid nothing, but some of the boys had some money. There was a trading-post, kept by Ward & Guerrier, about a mile from where our train had camped the night before. We had the idea we could buy some pack animals from them, to pack our stuff, and, being well armed, could proceed on foot. We sent a delegation of two of our boys up to Ward & Guerrier to see if they could buy some horses, but Ward & Guerrier refused to sell them any, even refused to sell them anything out of the trading-post, saying that Dan Patterson had left instructions not to sell us any horses or anything else, and not to allow us to camp anywhere near the trading post. He believed that we would be forced away from the post and would then be attacked by the Sioux and cleaned out, as, at that time, the Sioux were roaming over that whole country. When our boys returned and reported this condition of affairs, we held a consultation as to what was best to be done under the circumstances. The next morning each man took his load and started back on the road to Fort Laramie. This was in July, and the weather extremely hot and the sand in the road deep, so that traveling with a big load was anything but pleasant. With the load we had to carry we could not go over a quarter of a mile without stopping to rest, and we made camp early that day, put out a guard, cooked, ate and slept until next day.

The next morning we started on towards Fort Laramie again, carrying our loads and stopping to rest when we were tired. We kept close together and put in another night in camp on the river, using the same precautions as before. Next morning we broke camp and started for Fort Laramie, traveling under difficulties the same as before, until late in the afternoon, when, just as we came in sight of Fort Laramie, we met an emigrant train of some fifteen or twenty wagons, traveling west. The train was splendidly equipped and they were driving a lot of loose cattle. When we met them, the man in charge, who was an old German doctor, held a consultation with us, learned our condition, and as we were traveling through a hostile country, and we were well armed, they asked if we wanted to go on west, and we told them we did. Then they said they would haul our provisions and plunder if we would travel with them as guard against the Indians: that they had a number of milch cows, and we could have plenty of milk for the milking. We gladly accepted their offer and started with them. It was a German colony from Shelby county, Missouri, going through to Shoalwater Bay, Washington. We traveled with them till we got high up on the Sweetwater, out of the Sioux country. Then our company commenced falling in with other wagons and traveling on, until a man by the name of White and myself were finally left. I had been taken sick at the last crossing of the Sweetwater, and was unable to travel, so White remained with me. Several days later a party of four Mormons, with a four-horse wagon, who had been out prospecting on the Sweetwater (now in Wyoming), were returning to Salt Lake, and White made arrangements for them to take me to Salt Lake City. He paid them some little money that he had, and I gave them what blankets I had. When we arrived in Salt Lake City, which was about the 15th of August, 1855, I was in a very exhausted condition. At that time I had in my possession three half-dollars and two old-fashioned copper cents. White stayed on the Sweetwater to wait for some other train, and what became of him I never knew.

I stayed in Salt Lake City a day or two and finally met an old gentleman who was a Mormon, and who lived down in a ward known as Sugarhouse ward, south of the city. I do not recollect the manner of our meeting in the city, but do remember his asking where I was from. I told him North Carolina, and he said he was originally from somewhere in the western part of that

17

state. Seeing that I was in a weak condition, he said if I would go down to his place I could stop there for a week or two. He had a field of corn that the blackbirds were eating up, and said that if I would keep them off, I could have my board for my trouble. I readily accepted this proposition, and went home with the old Mormon and watched his patch of corn three or four days. In the meantime the old man had hauled down from the mountains some dead fir logs, hard and twisted, and he set me to scoring and hewing these logs for an addition to his house. I was not able to do this work, but kept at it a day or two and then said I thought I would travel. My possessions, at that time, consisted of an old oil-cloth carpet bag, with a few trinkets in it, among them a copy of Milton's Paradise Lost, which I had used at school. I left the old man and went on up to the city, stayed overnight, and then started north with the intention of striking the emigrant road near what is now the Idaho line, and trying to find some emigrants going to California. Just how I subsisted in getting up there, I do not now remember, but I do remember that when I arrived at the edge of the settlement, then called Willow Creek, now called the town of Willard, I stopped at a house and asked for some bread. They said they had none. There was a field of potatoes close to the house. I asked if I could have some, and they said to go and help myself. I dug some and putting them in my carpet sack started on and traveled until dark, when I came to a corral were there was a strawstack, in the outskirts of what is now Brigham City, I crawled into the strawstack and slept that night. Next morning I started on through Brigham City and when I came to a little stream I stopped and built a fire. I do not remember whether I had any matches or not, but I built a fire and roasted some of the potatoes and made my breakfast of potatoes, without salt. Starting on from there, in the forenoon of that day, I met a man with a wagon hauling a load of salt, that he had gathered up on the shores of Salt Lake. I asked if I could have some. He said, "Yes," and I took a handful of it. I then went on till some time in the afternoon. This was in the latter part of August. As I have before stated, I arrived in Salt Lake about the 15th of August. The road was very dusty and I was not very strong and was very tired. I met a man with a wagon load of old iron, old wagon tires and other iron from broken-down wagons. He stopped me and asked where I was going and I told him I was seeking the emigrant road, with the intention of joining some emigrant train and going with them to California. He said he had been out on the desert gathering up this old iron from broken-down wagons, that there were no emigrants, and that I could not get through to California. He said the Indians were bad on the Humboldt, and the emigrants had all passed. But he said if I would go back with him to Willow Creek, he would give me work. I considered the matter and concluded it was folly to proceed and got on to his wagon and rode back with him to Willow Creek. At that time my left arm had an abscess on it caused, I think, by the alkali water. I went back with him and the next day he put me to work doing some things around the place. Then the next day, I think it was, he set me and another man to making sun-dried brick or dobies. We had to walk about two miles from his house to make them. While I was with him, our living was anything but good. For breakfast we would have boiled potatoes, a little butter, some light bread and "coffee". Which was made from parched crusts of bread or roasted peas. When we went to work they gave us a bucket of skim milk and some bread, with a very little butter spread on it. That was our dinner. The work consisted of making these sun-dried bricks. There were three of us at the work. One made the mortar, another moulded the brick and I carried them into the yard. Two bricks, each on 12 inches long, about 6 inches wide and 4 inches thick, could be made in one mould. With that abscess on my arm and in my weakened condition, I put in the days from early dawn until late in the evening carrying bricks into the yard, and meantime living on that poor food. In two or three weeks we had made as many bricks as he wanted, and he said he wanted some charcoal burned. He was a blacksmith. Up on the side of the mountain about three miles there was a cove a depression in which there was some straggling timber, some rock maple, a very hard wood. I think for the work I did for him he paid me at the rate of $15 per month, giving me hickory shirts at $3 apiece. He said if I would go on the mountain and burn him some charcoal, and burning of which I had some knowledge, he would pay me 12 ½ cents a bushel and I board myself. I went up the mountain, cut that rock maple and burned charcoal there at 12 ½ cents per bushel, for about six weeks. I then came down to his house, having completed the job, and settled with him. In the meantime I had gotten a pair of pants made of elk-skin, for which he charged me $11, I think, one or two pairs of socks and a couple of hickory shirts, and he balanced the account with me, and said, as it was getting a little late, I had better look for some place to work for my board during the winter.

I then undertook to find a place where I could get my board for my work during the winter. My wardrobe, at that time, consisted of my elk-skin pants, two hickory shirts, no underwear, a couple of pairs of socks, my one pair of shoes and an old cloth coat, badly worn, and one hat, badly tattered and torn and of no use whatever. This was not a very good supply of clothing to stand the rigors of the Utah winter. I started out in the morning and traveled all day and in the evening found an Englishman and applied for work, asking if he would keep me during the winter for what work I could do for him. He told me to stop a few days and he would see what he could do for me. I stayed that night, and in the morning he yoked up his ox-team and said we would go out and get a load of fencing poles. We went up to the mountains some seven or eight miles, where the snow was deep, and got a load of poles and came home. I continued there three or four days, doing such work as he had for me to do, and living on such scant fare as the family provided; bread, a little butter, potatoes and pea coffee. Then he told me he could do nothing for me, and I had better seek some other place to winter. So after traveling all day again, I came to the house of a farmer, who lived about three miles south of Box Elder City. I told him my condition, and that I wanted some place to winter where I could pay for my board by such work as I could do. He told me he had but little house room, having only one house with one room in it, which answered for bedroom, living room, kitchen and dining room. He, however, told me to go over about a half mile to another farmer's house and see if I could stay there all night, and find out if Mr. Allen, which was the farmer's name, would keep me through the winter. If not, I was to come back in the morning and he would see what he could do. So I went over to Mr. Allen's and stayed all night there, stated to him my condition and what I wanted, and he told me that he could not keep me, that he had no work to do and was short of provisions. The next morning, after breakfast, I went back to the other house, which was kept by a Mr. William Tibbitts, a New York man. He was not in very good standing with the Mormon church, although he was a Mormon. The Mormons, in building the usual mud fort around the settlement in Box Elder, had levied an assessment on him, which he refused to pay, because he did not live within the city limits. The church authorities had taken two yoke of his cattle and sold them to pay his assessment for building this mud wall. This had angered him very much, and he was down on the Mormons and the Mormon church, although his wife was a staunch Mormon. He had a family of six children, all little girls, the eldest about 14 years of age and the next two old enough to go to school, but there was no school for them to go to. I told him I had been teaching school for two or three years, and we finally agreed that he should keep me that winter, and I should help him with his work and teach the little girls. For a sleeping apartment I was assigned to the granary, where I was furnished with a straw mattress and rather a slight quantity of bed clothing. I stayed with the old gentleman all that winter, doing such work as he had for me to do, going up the canyon with him, hauling out logs, and cutting and hewing them and helping him to put up an addition to his house. His wife was very kind to me, in fact very motherly. She took my old coat, tore it up, and out of the remains constructed a cap, which I wore during that winter. As I had no coat, she then took a piece of heavy Mormon-made cloth, containing about one and a half yards. This she put on my shoulders and put strings on it which were tied in front, and this I wore all winter in lieu of a coat. The family fared fairly well. There was plenty of bread, potatoes and meat and occasionally a cup of coffee. During the winter I taught his little girls the best I could with the limited supply of books he had, and remained there until along in early spring.

In the meantime I saw advertised in the Deseret News two letters for me in the post office at Salt Lake City; due on each of them five cents. Now I wanted those letters badly, but how to get them was a problem. Living about a quarter of a mile from Mr. Tibbitts was a family named Perry, from Missouri, who had come out in the fall of 1855, and bought the improvements on a piece of land. They were recent Mormon converts and Americans. In the same paper in which I saw my letters advertised there was also one advertised for Mrs. Perry with five cents due on it. It was 60 miles to Salt Lake City, and 15c postage to pay to get these three letters, and the trip to be made on foot, through snow from 12 to 18 inches deep and only a part of the road broken. That was a very severe winter in Utah and the snow had fallen very deep. In conversation with Mrs. Perry, she told me if I could manage to go to Salt Lake and get these letters she would give me half a dollar with which to pay the charges on them. I took the half dollar and started, and lived off of the Mormons on the road until I reached Salt Lake City, went to the post office and got the letters, the first I had received from home since early in the spring of the year before.

Now, I was in Salt Lake City with 35c in my pocket, an absolute stranger, and I had to eat and sleep, and how to procure these necessities I was at a loss to tell. In rambling around the city, I struck on three or four Americans, who had come in with an ox-train the fall before and who, stranded in the city, were living in an adobe building in the 19th ward. Getting into conversation with them, they found I was an American and a non-Mormon, and was, like themselves, stranded and destitute. They invited me to go to their house and partake of their hospitality while I was in the city, and I very cheerfully accepted the invitation. We went down to the house. All they had was the one room with a fireplace. No furniture excepting two or three stools, and no cooking utensils except a kettle and a skillet and a tin pan, and the supply of bedding was very limited. Along in the evening they proceeded to get the supper ready. They had some corn meal, which they mixed with cold water and baked in the skillet; we roasted potatoes in the hot ashes, and on this we made our supper. They were about destitute of money; had only about enough to pay their rent and buy a little cornmeal and a few potatoes. After supper, they said to me, "Now, you will have to go out and help to get wood for the night and morning." As Salt Lake City stood in a plain, with no timber within eight or ten miles, I naturally asked where we were to get it. They told me three or four of us would spread out and travel in different parts of the city, until he found good wood-piles, and then each would shoulder a load and bring it to the house. The city of Salt Lake is laid out in blocks of ten acres, so the blocks are large. I struck out on a street and traveled three or four blocks, until I came to a good, large woodpile, lying on the edge of the street. There I shouldered a dead cottonwood log, ten or twelve feet long, and of pretty good size. It was about all I could shoulder, although I was then robust and strong. After considerable labor I got it back to the house, where I found the other boys had each returned with a load of wood. And we had fuel enough to do us two or three days. But the devil would have been to pay had the Mormons caught me with that log on my shoulders. I stayed with these men two or three days and again started back to my wintering place. Just how I got back I hardly remember, but I lived upon the Mormons and foraged my way back to Mr. Tibbitts'.

I must digress here and tell a little about some of the privations that the Mormons suffered that winter. In the summer of 1855 the grasshoppers and crickets had eaten up the crops, and they were all on short rations that winter, and, to make matters worse, in the summer or fall of 1855 there had been a large emigration of English and Danish Mormons, that had come to Salt Lake. A large portion of the Danes had settled in Box Elder City, about three miles from where I was living. That winter was an unusually hard one and the snow very deep. At that time there was no settlement up in Cash valley (now one of the most populous valleys in Utah), and the church had there a herd of several thousand head of cattle. During the winter the snow was so deep that these cattle had to be driven out and down through Box Elder canyon, passing about a half mile from where I was stopping. They were being driven down to the shores of Salt Lake, where the snow was partly off. These cattle were so poor and starved that many of them fell and died while being driven, and a number of them lay down and died near where I was living. I saw the Danes in Box Elder come down in numbers, skin those poor cattle that had died of starvation and carry the meat back to their homes to live on.

During this winter my old shoes gave out and Mr. Tibbitts took me to Box Elder, to a shoemaker there, and had a pair of shoes made for me out of some Mormon-tanned leather. This leather was tough, but it was so porous that the water would come through it like a sieve. I remained with Mr. Tibbitts till along about the middle of April, when the snow had disappeared and the grass began to come up, and one day he said he had no further work for me, and that the best thing I could do would be to strike out and see if I could not find some place where I would get something for my work. I took his advice. Of course when I left, I had to leave this piece of cloth I had been wearing for a coat all winter, so I put on my extra hickory shirt, as I had two of them. Wearing my elk-skin pants, my socks, the old cap and the pair of shoes, I started out in high marching order, hardly knowing where to go, I took the road south towards Salt Lake City and traveled during that day. Where I stopped and whether I got anything to eat that night, I do not remember. Next morning I passed through the city of Ogden, and after walking two or three miles, I overtook two men who were traveling in the same direction. One of them had a single blanket, the other carried a rifle, shot-pouch and powder-horn. I enquired as to where they were going, told who I was, and where I was going. We found we were all in the same box. They had come in with a late freight train in the fall of 1855, and, having been paid off, they traveled to what was then known as Ogden Hole, now called North Ogden, and there struck a man by the name of Blodgett, with whom they made a contract to keep them until spring. They turned over what little money they had to him, how much I do not know, for which he was to board and lodge them till spring. One of these men was Jim Tingsley, from Indiana; the other, Sam Ballingee, a native of Kentucky who had been living a few years in Missouri. Jim thought it would help him to get through the winter if he joined the Mormon church. This he did, not in good faith, however, but merely thinking it would help him. They had stayed with this man Blodgett till the latter part of March, when Blodgett informed them their money was all used up and they would have to seek other quarters. So they took their one blanket and rifle and went down to the mouth of the Weber river, where it emptied into Salt Lake, and where there was a considerable quantity of box elder timber, and there they established a camp. There was a considerable number of wild geese coming in at that time, and as Sam was an excellent shot, they lived on wild geese in their camp there for about two weeks. Then they struck out to find better quarters, and were on their way when I overtook them. We held a consultation, and I might say formed a trust. Sam put in his rifle and pouch and powder-horn, Jim his blanket, and I, my experience. We had all heard that Dr. Hurt, U.S. Indian Agent for the Utah Indians, was opening a farm for the Indians on Spanish Fork river, about sixty miles south of Salt Lake City, and was employing some men. On consultation, we decided to try to reach that point, but it was about a hundred miles from where we were then, and then the problem came up as to how we were to subsist on that long journey. After some discussion, we agreed we would subsist on the Mormons by passing ourselves off as Mormons and begging our way. On the start, we drew straws to see who should make the attempt to get something to eat, and the first one to whom the lot fell to do this was to continue in that business during that day, then one of the rest was to do the same the succeeding day, and the other one on the third day. I think we were the first three original tramps in the United States, and we followed the methods very closely that are pursued by the tramps of the present day. My recollection is, it fell to Jim's lot to provide provisions and a sleeping place for the first day. The houses along the road were scattered, but we never passed one without asking for something to eat. Occasionally we would get a small piece of bread, but never any meat, that being an unknown quantity with us at the time. In this way we succeeded in getting enough bread to keep our hunger down to a certain extent and finding some place where we could lodge, which was usually in an outhouse. We passed on through Salt Lake City, and after walking about fifteen or twenty miles, we stopped one day, just for the purpose of trying to get something to eat. This was Jim's day to provide. We went to the house and found three or four ladies there and a number of children, but no man was to be seen. Now Jim had gall the equal of any man I ever saw. We went around to the kitchen and Jim told that we wanted something to eat. One of the ladies said they did not have anything to give us, that they were short of provisions themselves and people were traveling by all of the time and asking for something to eat. Jim stepped inside and sat down on a chair while Sam and I sat on the steps outside. Jim entered into familiar conservation with this lady, and tried to induce her to give us something to eat, but without any success. Again and again I attempted to urge him to come on, as I saw no prospect of our getting anything. Jim would say, "Don't be in any hurry; let's rest." There was a cooking stove in the room with a fire in it. We stopped there some little time, and finally, the lady opened the oven door and took out three or four loaves of bread, and with very ill grace, gave us a small loaf, which we took, and thanking her, started on. After we left I asked Jim, "What did you wait there so long for?" He said, "I knew that woman was baking bread, and I was going to stay there until she either took that bread out or burnt it up." We traveled on that afternoon and got to a place I think must have been American Fork, which was quite a settlement. Just before that, I said. "Where are we to stop tonight, Jim?" He replied. "We can go down to this settlement and stop with the bishop." I protested, telling him it was dangerous to stop with the bishop: as we were passing ourselves off as Mormons, he would be sure to put us through an examination, and we would be shown to be imposters and like as not we would be killed, as the Mormons were anything but friendly to the Gentiles. But Jim said, "That's all right, we can stand an examination; and then the bishops live better than anyone else." After dark we reached the settlement. At that time all these small Mormon settlements were surrounded with a high mud wall, a regular fort, and they were called forts. We approached the entrance and as we got to the gate, someone came out. Jim enquired if the bishop lived there, and was told that he did, but that he was not at home; he was at his farm about half a mile from there. Jim said "We will go up there." I still protested, but Jim insisted. "We will go up there and get something to eat." Finally, we found the bishop's house, halloed, and the bishop himself came out. We told him we were three travelers on our way to Spanish Fork, where we expected to get work for the government; that we wanted a place to stay all night and something to eat. The first questions he asked was, "Were we members of the church?" and of course we told him we were. After a slight hesitation he told us to come in and probably he could accommodate us. We went into the house. The family had just finished eating their supper. There were four women in there, his four wives, I suppose, and about a half-dozen children. Now, the Mormons at every meal ask a blessing and they have a stereotyped formula they use at all times, and generally wind up with, "God bless the Presidency of the Church, even Brother Brigham Amen." The bishop told the women to give us something to eat, and they put on the table some potatoes and a lot of meat, the first we had seen for a long time. We sat down to the table, and Jim, drawing down his face, asked the regulation stereotyped Mormon blessing, to which we both said "Amen," and then "fell to," and filled ourselves up. After we had eaten our meal, the old bishop, just as I expected, opened the racket, taking Jim first. Jim passed muster all right. Then came my turn. He asked me where I had lived? Where I was from? I told him. He then said, "When did you first hear about Mormonism?" I told him a good many years ago. He said, "Where did you first meet any of them?" I said, "Back in Mormon Grove, Kansas." It had happened that while we were herding cattle just back of Leavenworth, there was above that point a Mormon outfitting post, called Mormon Grove. I knew one of the bishops by the name of Snow, who was in charge of it. So when he asked me where I joined the Mormon church, I said, "At Mormon Grove." And when he asked who baptized me, I said, "Brother Snow." He turned to Sam, and he got through, too, in pretty good shape. We talked awhile, had family prayers, and we all said "Amen." Then he put us into a little lean-to, built of slabs and covered with slabs, and at one end of which there was one or two slabs missing, so the chickens could come in and out. There was a straw tick and an old quilt or two. It did not take us long to disrobe, for all we had to do was to take off our shoes. We then piled into bed and slept good and soundly. The next morning Jim was up first and made his toilet, which consisted of putting on his shoes, before Sam and I got up. He then commenced to rummage around the room. In one corner were two or three sacks of oats, and behind these he discovered a hen's nest with three eggs in it. He got the eggs out and commenced to break the shell and suck them. I remonstrated with him and pointed out that he would be sure to get us into trouble, but he said, "That's all right; they will never know the difference." So Jim swallowed the three eggs and put the shells back in the nest. We went to breakfast and the

30

old bishop asked the regulation blessing, to which we all said "Amen," as usual, and while we were eating, and Jim and the old man were keeping up an animated conversation, a little boy came into the room with those egg shells in his hand , and said; "Mamma, what do you suppose has sucked these eggs?" I was never so scared in my life, and I looked for some place to get into, but Jim never even blushed, and the woman said, "I guess it must be the cat sucked them." But the little boy said the cat did not make as big holes as that. I was so nervous that I was almost sweating blood. As we were getting ready to go the old Mormon said, "I wish you would see, if you can, that the government pays me for your entertainment last night." Jim promised faithfully to do so, and as Sam and I were anxious to get away, Jim finally broke loose and came on.

From there we went down to Spanish Fork and were hired by Dr. Hurt for the government at twenty dollars a month. They were building a dam and big canal to irrigate the farm they were making for the Indians on this greasewood land. The work was hard and we worked about twelve hours a day. For the first two or three weeks all we had to eat was beef and potatoes. We were allowed 2 ½ lbs. of beef and 2 ½ lbs, of potatoes for each man. But after being continually hungry for six or eight months, this did not satisfy us. We had no bread whatever. So, one day about eighty of us went up to the office. Dr. Hurt was not there, but there was an old gentleman by the name of Kerr, a good-natured old Virginian, in charge. He asked what was the matter and we told him we wanted something more to eat. He said, "Aren't you getting 2 ½ lbs. of meat and 2 ½ lbs. of potatoes each every day!" We told him we were, but that was not enough. He said, "How much do you think you could eat?" We told him we thought about 3 lbs.

each of potatoes and meat. He said, "Go to work; you shall have it." They issued us that ration for a couple of weeks, and by the end of that time we had gotten filled out and it was a little more than we wanted. By this time they had gotten a little cornmeal and added it to the rations of 2 ½ lbs. of beef and 2 ½ lbs. of potatoes. There was something over eighty men, divided into four messes. I was made the cook of one mess and Sam was made cook of another. In the meantime, we had drawn a little money and the Mormons were bringing in a little butter, and Sam and I, our messes being adjoining, bought two or three pounds of butter, and about this time they issued a small ration of flour, just enough to make one biscuit a day for each man, and we would cook the biscuits for supper. After Sam and I got this butter, we would make up our dough and pinch off enough to make about three biscuits for each of us, and would bake and eat them before the other boys came in, thus making their rations somewhat shorter, but as the most of them were Mormons, we were not particular about that.

We stayed there and worked for quite a while, when Ballingee and Tingsley got an opportunity to go with some parties who were going to California, but I stayed there and worked until the last of August, 1856, when a man by the name of Bill Madison, a Wisconsin man, and I quit, to go to Salt Lake City. We had an order on the firm of Hooper & Williams for our money, each having about fifty dollars coming. We had the idea of getting in with some emigrant train going to California. But when we arrived at Salt Lake City we found there was very little emigration that year and all of it had already passed; that the Indians had been unusually hostile down on the Humboldt and it was dangerous traveling. The only settlement in what is now Nevada was a small one on the Truckee river, just below the present town of Reno.

We stayed in Salt Lake City a few days, endeavoring to find some way of getting out of Utah. While we were there I saw five of the leading Danites, or, as they were called, "Destroying Angels." They were the notorious Porter Rockwell, the chief of the band, Lot Smith, Bill Hickman, Lot Huntington and Al Huntington.

After being in the city a few days I went one day to Hooper & Williams' store to draw a little of the money I had there, and saw Capt. Hooper, the senior member of the firm. He asked me if I could drive oxen and I told him, "Yes." He then asked me how I would like to take a trip out to the Flathead country. Now I had not the most remote idea where that country was, and so asked him, and he said, "Up north, on the headwaters of the Columbia river." He said there was a man in the city who wanted to go to the Flathead country, to trade with the Indians for horses, and wanted to take two ox-teams, and he wanted two ox-teamsters. He asked me how I would like to take such a trip, and I said, "I am willing to go anywhere to get out of this God-forsaken country." He said the man wanted two teamsters to go on the trip, and I told him there were two of us who would go. So he said to come down to the store that afternoon, and the man would be there. That afternoon we met the man, whose name was Van Etten, a Mormon. We made a bargain to drive teams for him to the Hell Gate river, in the Flathead country, five or six hundred miles north from Salt Lake City. He was to pay us fifteen dollars per month, and to sell us any goods we needed at Salt Lake prices, and we were to start within two or three days. The next day we commenced to get our wagons loaded, and everything ready for a start, and early in September, 1856, we left the city of the Saints and started on our journey to the Hell Gate river, in the Flathead country, which we found to be a point on the river about two miles below the present city of Missoula.

Our outfit consisted of two wagons loaded with goods for the Indian trade, each drawn by four yoke of oxen. The firm of Hooper & Williams sent in company with us, three wagons loaded with goods for the Indian trade, one wagon drawn by four mules and the other two each by four yoke of oxen. The Van Etten outfit consisted of himself and four men. The Hooper & Williams outfit consisted of six men. We traveled north up the east side of Salt Lake, crossed Bear river, near the point where the town of Corinne was afterwards located, on the Central Pacific railroad. We then continued on north, up the Malade valley and river to the head of that stream, and crossed Bannack mountain and followed down a stream called Bannack river, a tributary of Snake river. After following this stream for some distance, we left it and turned north to the Port Neuf river, which we crossed and continued on north until we reached Snake River at Fort Hall, an old Hudson's Bay Company trading post. We then followed up the left or south bank of the Snake river, six or seven miles, to a place where we found it could be forded with our wagons. We forded it, crossing to the north side of the stream. We followed up that stream to a point somewhere near where the town of Idaho Falls is now located. We then turned and traveled north by Market Lake, until we struck Medicine Lodge creek, at a point a short distance west of the present town of Dubois, on the Oregon Short Line railroad. We then followed up an Indian trail, along Medicine Lodge creek, to the summit of the Rocky mountains, which we crossed without any difficulty, and came down on what I believe was a tributary of Red Rock creek, now in the present county

34

of Beaverhead, in Montana. As near as I can remember, our entrance into what is now the State of Montana, was on or about the first of October, 1856. We then crossed Horse Prairie and Big Hole Prairie, and followed up a creek which I think is now called Trail creek, to the summit of the Continental Divide, which we crossed at what is now called Gibbon's Pass and came down into Ross' Hole, in the extreme upper end of Ravalli county. The road across the mountains at Gibbon's Pass was the most difficult piece of road over which we traveled throughout the entire journey. From the summit of the mountain down to Ross' Hole, was some two miles, with no road except an Indian trail, through the timber, and much of the way the descent was very steep, and in many places quite abrupt. In order to get our wagons down, it was necessary to lock both of the rear wheels and put rough-locks on them, by wrapping log chains around them, and also by hitching two yoke of cattle to the rear end of each wagon, with a man at their heads with a club, to make them pull back, and then came down the mountain at railroad speed. These were the second lot of wagons ever brought over this trail. In the fall of 1855, two or three wagons, lightly loaded, were brought over this trail, piloted by an old Mexican trapper named Emannuel Martin, generally known as and called "Old Manwell, the Spaniard."

From Ross' Hole we were compelled to make a detour, and cross another mountain, as there was no road down the canyon where the road is now established. After crossing this last mountain, we were in the Bitter Root valley, proper, and from that point had no great difficulty in getting our wagons through.

The first sign we had of habitation was at the mouth of Willow creek, just below the present town of Corvallis, where there were some log buildings, put up in the fall of 1853, for winter quarters, by Lieut. John Mullan, under orders of Gov. Isaac I. Stevens, the first Governor of the Territory of Washington. Stevens was making an exploration for a transcontinental railroad from St. Paul to Puget Sound, and directed Mullan to put up these buildings and with a small number of soldiers to remain there during the winter, for the purpose of getting acquainted with the Indians and to gain all possible knowledge of the country, climate, &c. These buildings were Cantonment Stevens. Some of these buildings were occupied by a man named Henry Brooks, who had charge of a number of horses and cattle belonging to a man named Neil McArthur, who had temporarily located at that place.

The next sign of a building that we saw was Fort Owen near the present town of Stevensville, which consisted of a log stockade, with some buildings inside. This was a trading post, established by Major John Owen. There were a few small log cabins built outside of the stockade and occupied by some Indians and half-breeds. There were only three white men at the Fort. Henri M. Chase was in charge of the place and the other two men were Al Tallman and Louis Robonin. All three of these men had been living in the Nez Perce country, near where the present town of Lewiston is now located, but in the summer of 1856, the Indians of that particular locality had become decidedly ugly, and these three men, with their Indian families, had come to the Bitter Root valley for the good of their health.

Major John Owen, the owner of the Fort, with a French-man named Pierre M. Lafontaine (now living in the Bitter Root valley), and a Delaware Indian called Delaware Jim, were absent from the Fort, having gone to Fort Benton for a supply of Indian goods. We arrived at the end of our journey on the Hell Gate river, about two miles below the present city of Missoula, about the 15th day of October, 1856.

At that time, there were encamped on the ground where the city of Missoula is now located, some 300 lodges of Indians, who were on their annual trip to the buffalo country, on the Yellowstone, Judith and Musselshell rivers and were waiting for these traders to arrive, to procure their supply of ammunition, blankets and other Indian goods. At that time the only places where buildings had been erected and were occupied by white people, within the limits of the present State of Montana, were those at Cantonment Stevens; Fort Owens, a small Catholic Mission, at the present site of St. Ignatius Mission: a few small buildings at the mouth of the Jocko river, where a temporary Indian Agency was established; Fort Benton; and Fort Union, near the mouth of the Yellowstone river. There was but one white woman in the entire country. Her name was Mrs. Minnie Miller, who, with her husband, was domiciled at the aforesaid Indian Agency.

The foregoing is a rambling statement, written from memory, of how I happened to come to Montana, with some of the incidents and difficulties which I encountered during that journey.

The reader will remember that I left the Missouri river at Leavenworth City early in June 1855, and, after sixteen months' wandering, I arrived in what is now the State of Montana, one of the grandest states in the Union.

As the readers of this narrative may wish to know what became of my two tramp partners, Sam Ballingee and James Tingsley, I will say that I do not know what became of Jim, the man with the superabundance of gall, but as for Sam Ballingee, he is now living, or was on the 15th day of November, 1909, in Lemhi county, Idaho, as I recently received a short letter from him, dated Carmen, Idaho, Nov. 15th, 1909, in which he said; "I well remember the night we stayed with old Brother Draper, and you and Jim asked the blessing."

From: Contributions to the Montana Historical Society, Vol. 7, 1910.

Notes:

The <u>Emigrant Trail</u> was used by many settlers in the mid 1800's to settle either in Oregon, California or Utah. Most started at a jumping-off point from the Missouri River then made their way west through Nebraska, then Wyoming to the town of South Pass. At this point, Mormon settlers made their way southwest to Utah. The rest continued on to Fort Hall, Idaho. At this point, the settlers either made their way southwest to California or northwest to Oregon. Judge Woody originally planned to go to California but ended up in western Montana.

A "hickory shirt" is also known as a "logger shirt" or "railroad shirt". It is made of a thick, striped cotton fabric similar to denim and is said to be as durable as hickory wood. These shirts are still available today and are used by workers who want durable clothing that is comfortable and cooling.

<u>Letter arrivals were posted in the newspaper</u> in the old west. Family members back east would send letters to the nearest post office to their loved ones. The post office would run newspaper announcements of the letters they received. The letter's recipients had to travel to the post office and pay the postage due before they got the letter.

The <u>Danites or Destroying Angels</u> were a vigilante group formed in 1838 by Mormons who lived in Missouri and Ohio.

Their name is said to come from a biblical prophecy in the Book of Daniel (Daniel 7:18). This prophecy said that the "Saints shall take the kingdom and possess it forever."

The Danites were originally meant to provide enforcement within the Mormon community but evolved into external defense as hostility from non-Mormons in Missouri increased. Under the leadership of Sampson Avard, they degenerated to looting from non-Mormons. He was removed from his post and excommunicated. Without Avard, the Danites continued their role as protectors of Mormons in Missouri until they moved to the Utah Territory.

In the Utah Territory, Brigham Young denied that the Danites still existed though they were said to take a role in the Utah War (1857-1858) where Mormons fought against armed forces of the U.S. Government. This time period was close to the time Judge Woody was in Utah, so, though Brigham Young denied their existence at that time, Judge Woody may well have seen Danites in Salt Lake City...especially since he could name five of them.

Judge Woody's route from Salt Lake City to Missoula is fairly easy to find in present day. For the most part, it follows present day Interstates and Highways. The first part of his journey is north on I-15 up until you reach Dillon, MT. There you go west on Highway 278 until Wisdom, MT. At Wisdom, go west on Highway 43 for about 25 miles until you see the turnoff for the Bitterroot Big Hole Road (FR 106) and turn north onto it. This road goes about 26.6 miles over Gibbon's Pass (incredibly rough and treacherous road) and ends up close to the Sula Ranger Station on US 93. Travel north on US 93. You will see the historical marker for Ross' Hole on the highway. Keep traveling north. You will pass Corvallis, the location of Cantonment Stevens though there is no trace of it now. Further north, you will reach Stevensville. Fort Owen State Park is located on the north side of town. Finally, you will reach the city of Missoula, Judge Woody's destination.

Judge Woody's First Christmas in Missoula Valley

This was back in 1956

GOOD TIME WITH THE BOYS

There Was No Superfluity of Luxuries. But They Just Enjoyed Themselves in the Snow-Covered Wilderness

"What did I do on the first Christmas I spent in Missoula?" said Judge Woody last night, repeating the question asked him by a STANDARD reporter. "Well, I hardly remember, it was so long ago. But I do recollect where I was and perhaps I can recall for you some of the incidents of the day."

Thereupon, the judge, becoming interested himself as the incidents of that long ago Christmas came back to him, told in graphic manner, the following story of the first Christmas ever spent by white men in the Missoula valley. It is impossible to present the story upon paper in the delightful way in which the narrator recited it, but the incidents are interesting and are, moreover, historical and are well worth presenting.

"It was Christmas, 1856," said the judge, "and I was camped on a beautiful wooded island of about 200 acres, which was at that time in the river almost exactly opposite the present residence of Frank Premo. It was

40

formed of a sort of slough, but it was covered with as fine timber as you ever laid eyes on and we were busy cutting it down. The island was known as Council Grove and was a historic spot. The year before we camped there, 1855, Governor Stephens had met the Flathead chief there in council and had signed with them the first treaty by which they ceded any portion of their lands to the United States. This was then a portion of Shoshone county, Washington, with the county seat at Fort Caldwell. Stevens was governor of the territory of Washington and ex officio superintendent of Indian Affairs. Our camp was in the middle of the grove, where the council had been held, and we slept in a big Indian lodge made of buffalo skins. It was a magnificent camp and the winter we spent there was a pleasant one.

"What was where the city of Missoula stands?" Nothing but snow on this Christmas day. It was snow, snow everywhere as far as eye could reach. There was nothing like a house nearer than Stevensville, where Major Owens had two or three cabins inside the enclosure now known as the 'adobe fort', which was then surrounded by a stockade. To the east, the nearest permanent habitation was at Fort Benton, and beyond that there was nothing until you got to old Fort Union at the mouth of the Yellowstone. There were also a few cabins up at St. Ignatius Mission, where the Jesuit fathers had even then located. But here in Missoula valley we were all alone and on this Christmas day we had not seen a white man for weeks, except the members of our own family.

"There were six of us, a man named Jackson, Bill Madison, Bill West, Jim Holt, myself and our employer, a Scotchman named MacArthur, an old Hudson Bay company man. We were getting out timber for a trading post which he proposed to build, but which was never

41

constructed. Despite the fact that we were alone, we had a merry time. The boys were a jolly, companionable lot of fellows and worked well together. Jackson, Madison and I were axemen, West did the hewing and Holt, who was an Englishman and couldn't use the axe, did the cooking. I don't know what become of the other men. I haven't heard of them for years.

"Bill West was the man who kept us laughing. He was a great, big, one-eyed fellow who hailed from Southwestern Missouri, where he had left a wife and sister of whom he was continually talking. He had the accent of a Louisiana buck negro and was the butt of the whole party. We called him 'Pork' and he answered to that name more readily than to his own. He gained that sobriquet when coming across the plains. As was customary on these long journeys, the men with the wagons paired off and West's partner was a man named Bean. The two so intimate that they gained the names of 'Pork' and 'Beans' and poor 'Pork's' name clung to him, even after 'Beans' had dropped from the party.

"We were well provisioned, having plenty of flour and bacon and beef and we could get from the Indians all the fish we wanted. On this Christmas day we worked part of the day---there was nothing else to do and took a part of the afternoon to rest in and dream of our homes in the East and the Christmas days that we had spent there in years gone by. I believe that Holt gave us a little extra dish for Christmas dinner, but the possibilities were not great and, though the dinner tasted good, it was not what would call a swell Christmas dinner by any means. One thing I do remember. We had nothing but water and coffee to drink. There was no Christmas punch and no egg nog, for we had no liquor in the camp. But there was a hearty good fellowship and cheer and, despite the conditions, that Christmas was a pleasant one. We told stories of our homes, and 'Pork' told us more about his wife and sister, until we laughed and laughed again. Our meals were laid upon a half cured buffalo hide, hard and stiff, spread upon the ground with the hair down. There was no linen and no silver, but it was a merry meal and we all enjoyed it. I think that it was at this dinner that 'Pork' looked up at our employer, MacArthur, who was as bald as a billiard cue and very sensitive, and said, 'Mister McArthur, you remind me of and uncle I had once.'

"'Do I? How's that?'"

"'He used to eat so much beef that his mouth and throat became coated with tallow, so we had to pour hot wata' on his head to melt the tallow and his hair all came off.'"

"Poor McArthur turned red and looked uncomfortable, but we all laughed so that he didn't turn West loose, as I feared he might. So the day went, and we enjoyed it fully. That was, as far as I know, the first Christmas ever spent by white men in this valley. I have spent a good many here since then, but none that were ever happier than this one."

December 1893

Note:

Council Grove State Park also known as "Grass Valley" where Judge Woody spent his first Christmas in Montana is located 8 miles west of Missoula off of Mullan Road.

Judge Woody's First New Year's Day in the Missoula Valley

"There was nothing particularly interesting about my first New Year's day in Missoula County, January 1, 1857", said Judge F. H. Woody yesterday. "There were five of us down in Grass valley, getting out timber. We were living in an Indian lodge and as I remember it, we spent the day out of the cold and snow. I cannot remember just how the day was spent, but, as our principal amusements were seven-up and reading. I suppose that's the way."

January 1, 1910

Note:

Seven-up was a card game. According to other reminiscences I've read from Judge Woody; books were a prime source of entertainment on the frontier. He related a tale of how he and his compatriots traveled long distances to obtain new books to read.

Judge Woody Falls Into a Reminiscent Mood

WAS COLD 42 YEARS AGO

Judge Woody became reminiscent the other night when somebody found fault with the cold weather. "Forty-two years ago on August 14," he said, "there was a heavy frost in this valley that destroyed all the wheat that had been sown that year. It was the first crop that was planted in this valley. I had helped to put it in early in the spring. It was on the land that is now embraced in the farm of Gaspard Deschamps in Grass valley. I worked for the two men who were trying to farm there until the early summer and then went up to Fort Owen to work. In August I joined a hunting party that was going to Deer Lodge valley and we started off with some half-breeds who were to go with us. I remember it was August 14 when we camped in this valley, and that night there was a white frost all over the low lands. The next day we went up on the canyon and two days later were at Garrison. That night ice half an inch thick formed in the camp where there was any standing water. The wheat that we had planted down at Grass valley was at that time 'in the milk', and the frost ruined it all. The smell from that field of wheat after the weather turned warm again was worse than the odor from a slaughter house. So, you see, this year is not the worst that has been experienced in this section and the statement that the climate is getting worse is not correct."

August 1899

FROM MISSOULA TO WALLA WALLA
IN 1857, ON HORSEBACK

In the fall (November) of the year 1857, I found myself in the Flathead Indian country, then in the Territory of Washington, where I had drifted with some Mormon Indian traders in October, 1856. At that time, 1856, there were in that country no white people except a few traders, a small Catholic Mission (the St. Ignatius), and a small Indian agency near the mouth of the Jocko river, and which was occupied by a man named Henry G. Miller and Minnie Miller, his wife, a white woman, she being the first white woman ever in the present State of Montana, and being the only white woman then in that country. Miller and his wife came from Utah in the summer 1856 and remained near the mouth of the Jocko river until the summer of 1857. I had remained in that country from about the middle of October, 1856, up to about the first of November, 1857, without seeing this white woman, or any other white woman during all of that time.

During all of the aforesaid time I had led something of a vagabond life, doing a little work for one or two of the Indian traders, and in hunting fishing and trapping with the Indians and half breeds. Late in the fall or 1857, I became tired of my isolation from the white settlements, and became quite anxious to again mix with people of my own race and color, but how to do so was a serious question. The nearest place inhabited by white people was at Fort Walla Walla, in the Walla Walla Valley, about five hundred miles west of the place where I was then living, and the country intervening, being an Indian country inhabited by different tribes of Indians, many of said tribes being anything but friendly to the whites, and some of them actually in a state of hostility.

In the early fall of 1857, two men, one named Hugh O'Neil, and the other named Ransey, came into the Flathead country from Colville, where they had been gold mining on the bars of the Columbia river. These men had been at Fort Walla Walla, and gave me a glowing account of that country, which made me more anxious to go there, but how to reach this land of promise was difficult to determine. About the first of November, 1857, I had occasion to visit the Catholic Mission at Saint Ignatius, some thirty-eight miles north of the place where I was then stopping, and while there, I met a lay brother of the Coeur d'Alene Mission, who had come up from the last named Mission with a number of large pack mules, and with several half-breed men and their wives to pack down to that Mission from the Saint Ignatius Mission, the wheels, axes, etc, of a couple of wagons, which were taken apart, and made into packs and loaded on the mules.

The said lay brother was a good natured old Irishman, named McGeen. Brother McGeen told me that if I wanted to go to Walla Walla that he was going to start from Saint Ignatius on a day certain, within the next week, and would take a short trail to the mouth of the St. Regis Deboris river where it joined the Bitter Root or Missoula river, and if I would meet him there on a day he named, I could travel with him and his half-breeds to the Coeur d'Alene Mission, and which would be on my direct way to Fort Walla Walla. The point of

47

meeting was about eighty miles down the Missoula river below where I was then staying.

I returned to my stopping place, fully determined to attempt the trip, full well considering the dangers to be encountered.

When the time came to make the start, it did not take a great while to make all necessary arrangements. I had two riding horses. On one of them I put a pack-saddle, and on it packed my small belongings, consisting of a single pair of blankets, a small quantity of bread and dried buffalo meat, a small flour sack containing two extra shirts, a few old letters, a few keepsakes from my distant home, a copy of Milton's Paradise Lost, and a few "ic-tas" with which to pay Indians for ferriage, etc.

Upon the other horse I placed my riding saddle, and I was then ready for my journey. I must not forget to mention my riding horse, for I remember him with gratitude and fond recollection for the noble service that he rendered me on the trip. He was a strawberry roan of Spanish breed, and was a horse formerly owned and ridden by Pearson, Governor Stevens' noted express rider, on his long trips from The Dalles to Fort Benton and other distant points in 1855, when Governor Stevens was holding councils and negotiating treaties with the various Indian tribes in the Northwest, and from this fact the horse was always known and called Pearson.

In those days we had no riding bridles, but rode our horses with a hair rope made by Indians of buffalo hair, the rope being placed around the lower jaw of the horse. My pack horse was led by a rope of the same kind placed around his nose and head in the form of a halter. Thus equipped, I commenced my long and dangerous journey, carrying no arms except one small butcher knife. The first day I travelled about forty miles and camped under a large pine tree without tent or fire.

I hobbled my horses and turned them out to feed, grass of the finest quality being plentiful. Early on the following morning I saddled up my horses and resumed my journey, and late in the afternoon arrived on the bank of the Missoula river, opposite the mouth of the Saint Regis De Borgia river, the place where I was to meet Brother McGeen and his Indian half-breeds with their pack animals. It seems that some mistake had been made as to the time of our starting, and that he had started one day earlier than he had intended, or that I had started one day too late, for we failed to meet at the designated point. I could see the remains of his camp fire on the opposite side of the river where he had encamped the night before, but not a man or horse was in sight.

The Missoula river at this point was, and is quite a large river, and fordable only at a very few places. I rode up and down the stream for a considerable distance, endeavoring to find the place where brother McGeen with his pack animals had crossed, but failed to find any sign of where they had entered the river. I then turned to the place where I had first reached the river, undetermined whether to attempt to cross the stream or return to again to my starting place in the Flathead country. I knew that it was a dangerous undertaking to attempt to cross, being alone. At the same time I did not want to retrace my steps, not knowing when I would have another opportunity to get out of that country. After deliberating on the matter for a short time, I determined to take the chances, and make the attempt to ford the river. I then took off all of my clothes except two woolen shirts, and tied them upon the top of my pack saddle, mounted my riding horse, leading my pack-horse, and started in.

At the place where I entered the water, it was quite shallow, but as I proceeded it gradually increased in depth, until I was about half way across the stream, where my horses struck swimming water. I kept my seat on my horse, until was about two-thirds of the way across the stream, when, to relieve my horse of his load so as to enable him to swim with greater ease, I slipped out of my saddle on the lower side of my horse into the ice-cold water, retaining my riding rope in my hand, and catching hold of his mane with my left hand, and at the same time letting loose of the rope with which I was leading my pack-horse, and in this way swam on the lower side of my riding horse until near the shore. At this point, the water was very deep and running up against a high cut bank. When my horse attempted to put his front feet on the bank, the water was so deep that his hind feet could not touch the bottom, and he reared up and fell back and came near falling upon me. I continued to hold on to my rope, and swam ashore, and then swam my horse down the stream until he found a place where he could land. I then led my horses up to the fire of logs left burning by the McGeen party, and dry wood being plentiful, I made a large fire and warmed and dried and dressed myself, unpacked and unsaddled my horses, hobbled them and turned them out to feed and made camp for the night, and after eating my supper of bread and dried meat, turned into my blankets, and slept as soundly as I ever did in the old farm house at my distant home down in "Dixie Land."

The next morning I made my breakfast on my bread and dried meat, packed and saddled my horses and started to overtake the McGeen party, which I did to my great relief before noon of that day.

I travelled with the party until we reached the Coeur d'Alene Mission, which took us from the crossing of the river about five or six days. Our way followed an old Indian trail which led up the Saint Regis river, crossing it many times, and which, for the most of the way, was through a forest of heavy pine, tamarack and cedar timber, and was obstructed by fallen timber, much of it of very large trees. I have seen many Indian trails, but never one so bad as this one. After following this trail for a long distance up the Saint Regis river, we left the river and crossed over the mountain on to the Coeur d'Alene river, and followed that stream down to the Mission. From the time I overtook the McGeen party until we reached the Mission, it snowed and rained nearly all of the time. The party had with them two small buffalo skin Indian lodges, in which we slept at night, which was some comfort.

Arriving at the Coeur d'Alene Mission, I was very hospitably received by the fathers then there, and I remained there two or three days to rest and recruit myself for the remainder and most dangerous part of my journey. I counselled with the fathers as to the best course to take, and they endeavored to tell me the route to take, and advised me to hire an Indian at the Mission to guide me to Snake river, and at a point above the Palouse Crossing. As I had two horses with me, I finally made a bargain with a Coeur d'Alene Indian to act as my guide, giving him one of my horses for so doing. Here I made a mistake in then and there turning the horse over to the Indian, and trusting to his honesty to do as he agreed to do. I obtained from the fathers at the Mission some bread, the shank-bone of a ham and some dried salmon, and tied my belongings and provisions on behind my riding saddle, and with my Indian guide, resumed my journey. That night we camped at a small prairie in the mountains, called "Wolf's Lodge", and the next day about noon, arrived at the foot of the Coeur d'Alene Lake, about where Fort Sherman was afterward located, where we found eight or ten lodges of Coeur d'Alene Indians in camp. Here my guide told me he could go no further, as one of his children back at the Mission was sick, and that he must return, but said he would get his brother to go on with me. After a long parley with his brother, the brother agreed to go, but had to go out on the range and get his horse. After a long delay he procured his horse, and announced himself ready to proceed. I did not like this arrangement, but as the Indian had my horse, I was forced to submit to the change of guides. We started from the Indian camp and went down the Spokane river two or three miles, and then crossed it by fording. At that time it was nearly night and time to camp. The Indian said some of his people were camped a short distance from the river, and that we would go to their camp and stay all night with them, and I, seeing nothing better, agreed to his suggestion. About one or two miles from the river, we found five or six lodges of Coeur d'Alene Indians. We rode up to the lodge of the chief, and my guide and he talked a little while, and the chief then told us to get off of our horses and unsaddle them, and he then gave them to an Indian boy to take out and put them in the Indian herd of horses and then invited us into his lodge. The first thing after going to the lodge was to have a smoke Indian fashion, passing the pipe from one to another from right to left, each person taking two or three draws, and then passing it to the person sitting next to him on his left. He then directed his squaw to get us some supper, which she did by baking some bread out of some coarse flour from the Mission, and giving us the bread, some dried salmon and cooked camas roots. The first thing after we had eaten our supper was to have another smoke. After the smoke was ended, the chief asked me what I had in a small flour sack that I had; when I told him he directed me to empty out its contents that he might see what was in it, and, of course, I complied with his request, as it would have been folly to have refused.

When I placed the contents on a buffalo robe, and he saw several letters, old and badly worn by carriage, he asked me what they were. I gave him to understand that they were old letters that I had received from my people back in the States, and seeing that they were old and much worn, he evidently believed me, and directed me to put all of the things back into the sack. He then told me the reason why he had made me show him what I had in the sack. He said that there were a lot of white men at Fort Colville, and also soldiers at Walla Walla, and that the chief of the Colville Indians had told him that if any white men passed through his country to search them and see if they were carrying any letters from soldiers at one place to the white men at the other place, and if they had any to take them from them.

The next morning we had a breakfast similar to the supper of the night before. Our horses were brought in, and we saddled up and resumed our journey. It was quite cloudy, and soon after we started commenced snowing lightly, but melted as it fell. We followed a very dim old Indian trail through a hilly country, sparsely timbered with pine trees. Some time after noon, we came to a lake, and as I now remember, it was rather a narrow lake between a quarter and a half mile wide and something more than a mile long. We followed down the side of it where we first struck it to the other end. Where we first struck it, the shores of it were rough and rocky, but when we reached the other end of it, it terminated in a rather sandy plain. Here we found where ten or fifteen lodges of Indians had been encamped, and from the indications that we saw, it appeared as though the Indians had moved from the place quite recently. I asked my guide what Indians they were that had been encamped there, and he said he did not know. Said that maybe they were Spokanes or Palouses, "and if they are Palouses and catch us they will kill you, but if they kill you, they will kill me, too." This was not very consoling to me. I did not care very much if they killed my guide, but I did not really want to be killed. Some times in the following night, I was only sorry that they did not catch and kill my guide, as he really needed killing.

At the lower end of this lake, where the Indians had been encamped there was a plain, well-worn old Indian trail, which we followed. Immediately after leaving this old Indian encampment, and in the trail which we were following, I saw something which was then a puzzle to me, and it was a puzzle that I have never been able to solve. In the trail leading from the Indian camp, were the tracks of a white man, who evidently wore a No. 10 shoe, and a rather light make of shoe. The tracks had the appearance of being quite recently made. What white man could possibly have been on foot in the country at that time was something I could not then understand, nor have I ever been able to fathom the mystery. That the tracks were made by a white man was plainly evident by the way the man walked. There were never made by an Indian. We followed this trail, leading, as I supposed in the direction of Snake river, the man's track still appearing in the trail, going in the same direction that we were going. When I left the Coeur d'Alene Mission the fathers told me that there was a well known landmark called St. Joseph's Mountain, to the right of which I should go. After we left the lake we commenced to go up onto an elevated prairie. It was very cloudy, and we could tell nothing about the points of the compass. A short time before night, the guide stopped and said we must have a smoke, and after we had smoked, he told me to untie a white blanket that was tied on behind my saddle, and I did as he requested. He took the blanket and spread it out on the ground, gathered up a little snow that had remained in the roots of the bunch grass, and poured a little gunpowder into his hand on the snow and made a black mixture, and then took the blanket and with the paint made a rough map on it, showing the way we should go, at the same time claiming that one of his children was sick, and that he wanted to go back home. I told him he must go on the Snake river. I could see that he was not in a good humor. We mounted our horses and rode on until nearly dark, when we came to a creek, with a few quite large pine trees standing near the stream, and here we camped. We unsaddled our horses, hobbled them and turned them out to feed. We then built a small fire, ate our scant supper, had a smoke and rolled up in our blankets and went to sleep. I rolled up in my blanket and went to sleep under one of the pine trees, and the guide did likewise, but at some little distance from me. I slept quite soundly until probably some time after midnight, when I woke up, and found my horse standing beside me and the Indian and his horse gone, the scoundrel having deliberately deserted me. I looked around, but could find no trace of the Indian or his horse. I went to sleep again, and slept soundly until morning, when I ate my scanty breakfast, saddled my horse and resumed my journey. After crossing the creek I again saw this white man's track in the trail. After going two or three miles, I came to a dry valley about a half a mile wide, and as I remember it, leading off down to my right, with a large number of

Indian trails running parallel with each other, and worn down deep, and here I lost all trace of the white man's track. Looking down this valley, I saw large bands of horses, and believing that these trails led down to the Palouse Crossing, which I was endeavoring to avoid, I crossed over them, and took to the prairie without any trail, going in the direction which I believed would lead me to Snake river. I was going up all the time in an elevated grass country, and about noon I came to a spring in the hills, and stopped, watered my horse, and ate my lunch. After resting myself and horse, I resumed my journey, and just about sundown (it having cleared up partially), I arrived on top of a hill on the prairie, from which point I could see a piece of water far down below me. I was at a loss to tell if it was Snake river, or a small lake. Nevertheless, I started down the hill toward it, as I needed some water, as did also my horse. After going some distance, I could hear the water roaring; Then I was satisfied that it was no lake, and as I know in reason, there could be no other river there than the Snake, I felt better. I proceeded down towards the river, following a small ravine that led down to the river. Just as I reached the mouth of the ravine, at a point where an Indian trail passed up the river, I very unexpectedly met an Indian and a squaw coming on the trail going up the river. They seemed as surprised as I was, and the Indian, who could talk a little English, and a smattering of Chinook jargon, hailed me with the usual salutation of "How," and I replied in the same manner. He asked me from whence I came, and I told him from the Flathead country. He then asked me where I was going, and I told him to Walla Walla. He then asked me if I was alone, and I put on a bold face and told him "No." that there was a party of about fifteen white men with me who were a short distance behind.

He then told me there was a camp of some eight or ten lodges of Nez Perce Indians camped a short distance down the river, and told me to go down and camp with them, which I promised to do, without, however, intending to do so. The Indian and his squaw then rode on up the trail and I rode down to the river and watered my horse and obtained a drink myself, and waited and watched the two Indians go up the river about a half a mile, where they camped, turned their horses loose, and built a fire. I then returned to the mouth of the ravine, down which I had come, and rode back up it about a quarter of a mile, and turned up on a small depression of the prairie, and went into camp. I unsaddled my horse and turned him loose to feed. I then made a meal on my small stock of provisions, and after letting my horse feed a while, I spread down my blankets and prepared to go to sleep, but before doing so I brought my horse up near my bed, and with my hair rope put a halter on him, and tied the other end of the rope around my waist and went to sleep, and slept as sound as I ever did in my life. In the morning early, I arose, ate my breakfast out of my fast disappearing commissary, saddled my horse and started down toward the river, intending to ride down to the Indian camp and get them to put me over the river, as I knew that all of the Indians on the lower part of Snake river had good canoes. I rode to the camp and rode up to the lodge of the chief, and asked him to have some one take a canoe and put me over the river, but he absolutely refused, and told me to swim it, which to my mind was an impossibility to do. I was in a quandary, as I had reason to believe that I was only a short distance above the Palouse crossing, which I was endeavoring to avoid, believing that if I went there I would in all probability be killed. Here I was in a dilemma, as I did not want to retrace my steps back to the Coeur d'Alene Mission, and the only show I had was to cross the river, but how to do it was the question. However, I soon made up my mind to take a desperate chance, and attempt to cross. I noticed that there was considerable driftwood on the banks of the river, an at that point there was very little current in stream, and as I had two hair ropes with me I determined to get two large sticks of driftwood and lash them together so as to make a raft, turn my horse loose and make him swim, and attempt to cross on my raft, a decidedly dangerous and desperate undertaking. While looking for a good place to make the attempt, I came on to two Indian boys with a large canoe gathering driftwood on the bank of the stream. I rode up to them and after taking a look at them saw that they were slaves---this I could tell from the fact that their hair had been cut short. I had seen the Nez Perce Indians passing through the Flathead country going to the buffalo country and had noticed Indians of the description with them, and learned that they were slaves, being captives taken in southern Oregon and California, and when captured their hair was cut short, and kept cut in that manner. I rode up to them and asked them to put me over the river, offering them some Indian goods which I had brought with me, consisting of a few yards of calico, Indian paint, brass tacks, etc., which I had brought with me to trade to Indians for ferriage and provisions. I showed them the goods and offered them all I had if they would put me over. At first they absolutely refused, but after talking with each other, one of them went around a bend in the river, evidently to see if they put me over if they would be seen from the Indian lodges above. When he came back they held a short conversation between themselves, and then made signs that they would cross me. They took my saddle and little pack off my horse and put them in the canoe, and told me to get it, and started across leading my horse, he swimming below the canoe. In a few minutes we were over and a happier tenderfoot you never saw. I saddled up and started without any trail, and when I climbed to the top of the hill, I looked down the river and saw an Indian camp about three or four miles below the point where I crossed.

I travelled all that day in the direction, as I supposed of Fort Walla Walla, and over a high grass covered country, devoid of trees, streams or trails, and at night camped at a spring that I found in the hills. The next morning the country was covered with a very heavy fog, that continued nearly all that day. After traveling some distance I fell into a large Indian trail, and later in the day saw through the fog, the tops of trees, and soon came to a stream of water, which I have since learned was the Touchet river. Here I stopped and let my horse rest and feed for a while, while I consumed the remainder of my provisions.

Before leaving the Flathead country the men, O'Neil and Ramsey, had told me that the soldiers at Fort Walla Walla had been in the habit of making hay out on Dry Creek, some six or seven miles from the Fort.

After resting my horse, I resumed my journey, still following the Indian trail, and after going some distance I again saw some trees, and on arriving at them found a stream, or the bed of a stream, but do not now remember whether or not there was any water in it. After passing over this stream for a short distance, I saw where some person had been cutting grass, and going a little further I found wagon tracks were some persons had been hauling hay. I then knew that I was near the promised land, and a happier mortal never lived.

By this time the fog had lifted and I was enabled to see for quite a distance. I rode on a few miles, and saw a band of horses off some distance from the trail. The horses looked to be too large for Indian horses, and as I drew nearer to them, I saw two mounted men, apparently herding them. I rode towards them and soon discovered that the two men wore blue overcoats. I rode up to them, and found that they were two soldiers herding dragoon horses. Then I felt that my troubles and fears for personal safety were all over. I asked them how far it was to the Fort, and they told me about two miles. I rode on and soon came in sight of the Dragoon Cantonment, and as I came to Mill Creek, just above the Suttler's Store. I met Col. William Craig, Henry G. Miller and William Scott. I had a letter for Col. Craig, which hand been given me by Henri M. Chase, which I handed to Col. Craig, and, after reading it, he told me the road leading to his house, about one mile distant, and told me to go there and stop, and that he would soon be at home. I went to the house, turned my horse out and prepared to take a rest, being nearly tired out, and that night had the first good square meal, the first that I had had for many days, and to which I did full justice. This ended one of the most venturesome and dangerous journeys ever taken by a young tenderfoot.

NOTE---I went to Spokane in August, 1911, and went out to Liberty Lake, some twelve miles from the City of Spokane, and feel satisfied that the lake that I found on my journey was Liberty Lake, and as I crossed no stream after leaving the lake, except the stream on which I camped when my Indian guide left me, I am constrained to believe that stream was what is now called "Hangman's Creek."

FRANK H. WOODY
December 1912

Notes:

The route Judge Woody took from the Missoula (Hell's Gate) valley to Fort Walla Walla can be closely approximated using present day roads. His route from Missoula to Spokane was basically the same path as I-90 which follows a well-used Indian trail. From Spokane he traveled south approximately on the path of Highway 195, then west on Highway 26, then southwest on Highway 127, then south on Highway 12 to Walla Walla.

The Coeur d'Alene Mission is present day Cataldo Mission, 25 miles east of Coeur d'Alene.

HELL GATE'S DEATH RATE

By Arthur L. Stone

When the afternoon sun illumines the entrance to Hell Gate canyon, the scene is remarkably beautiful. This canyon is one of the natural gateways through the mountains; its walls rise abruptly from the level floor, their lines softened by their covering of trees; all day these blankets of pine and fir and tamarack lie dark and somber upon their steep-pitched resting places; the dense green is almost black in the shadow of Mount Sentinel.   But when the afternoon sun turns its searchlight into the canyon's opening, it reveals new beauties; new lines spring into sight; new details become visible and the green-black forest takes on a multitude of hues, blending beautifully into a perfect chromatic scheme.   Beholding this transformation, the visitor in this scene wonders regarding the derivation of the forbidding name of this canyon entrance. In an earlier story I have told how the name originated; it was not the appearance of this gateway which suggested the appellation; it came from the bloody Indian history which was written there.   But as the beholder gazes at the entrancingly beautiful scene which spreads before him as he looks into the canyon, he regrets that it does not bear a designation more in keeping with its rare beauty.

And so it is with the valley which derived its former name from this canyon entrance. Singularly beautiful is this basin, hemmed in by inspiring mountains, watered by charming streams and decked

62

with great stretches of meadow and rolling prairie. "Hell Gate ronde," it was called by the early settlers, and it retained this name until the growth of Missoula forced a change in the nomenclature, giving a name not dissimilar in its derivation and original significance, but certainly more musical in sound. It is truly a beautiful valley which reaches from the canyon's mouth, where the waters of the Rattlesnake and the Missoula mingle, away to where the Bitter Root ripples along in the shadow of Lolo mountain and westward to where the blue waters of Nine Mile flow over their golden sands to add to the tide of the greater stream which runs on to the ocean. But this valley used to be known as the Hell Gate and that, also, was the name which was borne by the first town builded upon its gentle slope.

Fair it is now — this valley — and fair it was to look upon when the white men first beheld it. Each of the early visitors to this region wrote eloquently of the charm of this basin. Each described its beauty, dwelling upon the loveliness of its streams, the grandeur of its mountain walls and the fertility of its fields. It was here that the Selish chiefs met in council with Governor Stevens; it was here that old Chief Victor stood and claimed the valley as the center of his tribal domain. Here camped the Selish tribes on their way eastward to the buffalo grounds — camped for barter and for rest. Here they camped on their way back, for recuperation if worsted and for celebration if victorious in their eastern sorties. It had been a favorite meeting place for the kindred tribes. It was the center of their hereditary domain. Unimpressionable we are wont to regard the Indian, but we find that he always chose his camping places where beauty of surroundings appeals to us now — and it must have appealed to him, unconsciously, perhaps, but strongly nevertheless.

But if there is much in the appearance of this valley that makes the name seem incongruous, there is much in the history of the old town of Hell Gate that makes it seem singularly appropriate, even as the Indian history of the old trail up the canyon made the name fit there. Hell Gate was founded as a white settlement in 1860. It retained its identity until 1865. During its existence its maximum population was 14 — the average was 12 — but in the months that it was doing business there were no less than nine men who died there with their boots on. For them, surely, it was the entrance to Hades, though the growl of Cerberus took the form of the bark of a Colt's army gun.

There is not much left to mark the site of the first town in this valley. Two or three of its buildings remain; they are out-houses now of a prosperous ranch. There is no trace of its single street. A guide is necessary to locate the buildings. Four mounds were there until a few years ago, which marked the resting places of the last of the victims of the righteous wrath of the Montana Vigilantes. But now even these have disappeared before the leveling influence of the wheat-farmer's plow. Unless you know the corner of the old rail fence in which they were planted, you cannot locate now the place where these offenders against pioneer law were hustled when they were cut down from their impromptu gallows.

It was in August, 1860, that Frank L. Worden and Christopher P. Higgins, partners under the firm name of Worden & Company, armed with a sutler's license to trade with the Indians, came from Walla Walla, with a pack train bearing a stock of merchandise and established the town of Hell Gate. They had intended to locate near Fort Owen in the Bitter Root, but they found that the government was then engaged in establishing an agency at Jocko — the present reservation headquarters. They didn't like to go to either of the Indian headquarters for fear of losing the business of the other, so they settled upon the location at Hell Gate, midway between the two. And so the little town was started.

Judge Frank H. Woody, who had been in the employ of Worden at Walla Walla, came with the outfit from the coast and participated in the establishment of the town. The first store was opened in a tent. It was August and the tent was comfortable enough; but immediate preparations had to be made for the approaching winter and the partners began to skirmish about for logs for building material. Prospecting about the country, they found David Pattee living with Captain Grant on what is now the county road, two miles west of Missoula's present location. Pattee had got out and hewed a set of cottonwood logs for building a house for himself. The logs were framed for a building 16 feet by 18 and they were bought on the spot, Pattee agreeing to deliver them at the place where was erected the first building in Hell Gate.

Pattee fulfilled the terms of his contract and Woody and a Frenchman — Narcisse Sanpar — erected the building, making the roof of poles covered with sods. That building yet stands near the county road to Frenchtown. It was the first store or trading post built within the present limits of the county of Missoula. In fact, it was the first mercantile establishment in western Montana, except the post at Fort Owen, near what is now Stevensville, and the old Hudson Bay company post, where Angus McDonald had headquarters on Post creek, six miles the other side of St. Ignatius mission. When Hell Gate was founded, it was in the territory of Washington. Afterward, it was in Idaho; later, it was in the territory of Montana. It had a lively set of changes as to post office address, but it remained stationary as to location.

This little log cabin was the only structure erected that year. In 1861, Worden & Company built another store and W. B. S. Higgins erected a building which was used as a residence. In the autumn of 1861, P. J. Bolte built a little house which he used as a saloon. In 1863 there was a blacksmith shop added to the collection of houses; Judge Woody thinks it was built by Henry Buckhouse; his is the only information which is available. In 1864, Woodward & Clements brought in a stock of merchandise and started an opposition store. That same summer J. P. Shockley built a house which was used as a boarding house. This constituted the entire architectural strength of the town of Hell Gate.

But, though the town was small, it was active. There was something doing there all the time. I have heard from Judge Woody and others of those who were of the Hell Gate population and from them I have learned a good many interesting incidents of the life in this pioneer town. There is good material for a "trail" story in the early merchandising experiences of these days. But this story will deal with the remarkable death rate of the town of Hell Gate.

It should not be inferred that the climate of Hell Gate ronde was not salubrious; there was no malaria in the air; there were no bacilli in the streams; there were no lurking germs to prey upon the pioneers. Death did not lurk in any of these insidious forms in Hell Gate. The dark angel's work was all done in the open.

Bolte's saloon, opened in 1861, didn't last very long. Bolte went out of business the following year. This furnishes reasonable evidence that John Barleycorn had comparatively little to do with the death rate which is the really remarkable feature of the history of Hell Gate. When Bolte closed his bar, there was no saloon in Hell Gate for more than a year. In 1863 a stranger came to town, giving the name of Cyrus Skinner. He bought a stock of booze and opened a saloon in the old Bolte building. His place became the loafing place of some tough-looking characters who followed him to the town and was never a popular resort. He kept his establishment going, however, until one dark night in January, 1864, when he went out of business suddenly and his going started the boom in Hell Gate's death rate.

On this dark night, aforesaid, the quiet of Hell Gate was disturbed by the sound of galloping hoofs. There was an arrival in town. It was a party which was made up of a delegation of Vigilantes from Virginia City. The arrival was unheralded, but the visitors lost no time in introducing themselves and in stating their business. When they had presented their credentials and had held a brief parley, Cyrus Skinner and two of his loitering companions, Alex Carter and Johnnie Cooper, were dangling from a pole which had been fastened into a log corral in the lower part of town. Continuing their rapid ride across the valley and up the trail into the Coriacan defile, the Vigilantes stopped at the O'Keefe ranch and located Bob Zachery, who was brought to Hell Gate and hanged there alongside the others. Baron O'Keefe having entered violent protests against an execution on his ranch. This was the last Vigilante execution in Montana.

A couple of months later, in March, Hell Gate's death rate received another boost. This time the affair was a home production. The Hell Gate people and the farmers in the valley had become alarmed by the actions of a couple of young Indians who were known to have killed a prospector named Ward in the canyon near where the town of Clinton now stands. They had become offensive and had attacked a Frenchman in the Coriacan defile. They were boldly insolent and were threatening an uprising of the reds. The settlers around Hell Gate dispatched Milton W. Tipton, a farmer living near Frenchtown, to Alder gulch with an appeal to the miners at Virginia City for assistance. The Indians soon learned of this move and it became their turn to be alarmed. They knew it meant trouble if the miners came down to fight. The chief of the Pend d'Oreilles was the father of the chief offender and, upon the demand of his people, he delivered his son to the Hell Gate people. The young Indian was brought in, tied and disgraced. The Hell Gate men led him to the pole which had served as gallows for the road agents and the old corral was once more decorated with a dangling human form. Hell Gate's death list had reached a total of five.

In the autumn of 1864, a man named Crow, who had been loafing about the village with no apparent means of support, was shot and killed by Matt Craft at the tent which was Craft's home, about a quarter of a mile above the Worden store. Craft claimed that Crow had come to the tent and had insulted Mrs. Craft. This statement was accepted. There were no officers of the law in the country and nothing was done to the shooter. The death list totaled six.

The visit of the Vigilantes had closed Hell Gate's saloon and it was not reopened until the fall of 1864, when William Cook stocked the old building with liquors and conducted a place which became a popular resort for men who were traveling back and forth between Fort Owen and Jocko. Everybody played poker in those days and there was almost always a game in progress at Cook's place. One afternoon two Irishmen had come to Cook's and had played cards until nearly dark. They became involved in a quarrel over the settlement of their game. A matter of $2.50 was the issue and they left the saloon wrangling about it.

There were no electric lights in Hell Gate. The illumination of the rough interior came from a big fireplace in one side of the room and from candles stuck about. On the night of the day that the Irishmen, McLaughlin and Doran, had quarreled over their cards, there were some of the Hell Gate men seated at a table in front of the fireplace, playing a friendly game, when the two returned — they were quarreling. That night added two more names to the list of Hell Gate's dead. One of the men who sat at the little table has told me this story of the spectacular events of that evening:

"We were playing at a little table near the fireplace, from which we got most of our light. We had also a candle on the table. Doran had walked over to our side of the room and stood with his back to the fire. McLaughlin, who had been an employee at the Jocko agency, was sitting on a whisky barrel, leaning against a brandy keg. He had evidently apprehended trouble, for he had borrowed a big navy pistol from Captain Higgins. He wore an old blue army overcoat and, though we didn't know it, had the gun in his lap under the cape of the coat.

"The men came into Cook's quarreling and they continued their argument. They were not talking very loud, but seemed very much in earnest. Standing in front of the fire, Doran reached for his hip under his coat, evidently to draw his pistol. McLaughlin leaped to his feet, exclaiming, 'I've a pistol as well as yez.' He threw back the cape of his coat. There were two flashes at the same instant. All the candles were extinguished and the close of the tragedy was enacted in the fitful light from the fireplace.

"At the table, we jumped up. The men were firing across the way to the front door and we couldn't get out that way. But we wanted mighty bad to get out. There was a thin board partition across the back of the room, separating Cook's living quarters from the saloon. Through this we dashed. I was in the lead. We upset a sheet iron stove which was in the living room; we scared Cook's half breed wife and her baby and they screamed; the discharge of the pistols sounded like artillery—it was the greatest confusion I ever knew.

"Reaching the back door, the others pressed so hard against me that I couldn't swing the door. While I was struggling with it, Cook came out and said 'I can open it. Go tell Captain Higgins I am shot.' I hurried to the store. Higgins returned with me and we met two men supporting Cook, who was hardly able to move. The shooting was all over. McLaughlin had fired but one shot. Doran had continued his bombardment until he was out of ammunition. He had fled and there was darkness and silence when we returned with our burden.

"Cook was laid upon the counter and an examination showed that a bullet had passed through his body, entering above the left hip and lodging right under the skin on the side. Captain Higgins used a razor to extract the bullet, but that was about all we could do. There was no doctor and no means of cleaning the wound. We placed poor Cook in his bed and he died Thursday. Everything we could do was done for him. Father Grassi came up from Frenchtown to see him, but said the shot had pierced the bowels and it was a hopeless case. Cook was buried near the little church which Father Grassi had built just below Hell Gate.

"This made the death list eight. McLaughlin had died almost immediately; when found he had crawled to the back room in Cook's and was breathing his last. Doran fled across the river on the ice and made his way to Stevensville. There was a supposed justice of the peace there, Roop by name, and there was the mere form of a hearing before him. Despite the testimony of John Chatfield, who was one of the party playing cards in Cook's when the shooting occurred, Doran was released. He went over to Madison county then. Oldtimers report having seen him in Stevensville and Hamilton this summer. To one of them at least he mentioned his identity and referred to Hell Gate incidents.

The last chapter in the mortuary record of Hell Gate was written in the early spring of 1865, when J. P. Shockley deliberately shot himself with a pistol at his own home, which has been mentioned as the last house built in the town. His death made the total list number nine, which was a fairly good record for a town of 14 people in two years. There were no other deaths in the town. Its people were strong and healthy. Those of them who died, died quickly and without the preliminary of being sick. There is, as far as I can find, no trace of the little burying ground of Hell Gate. There were five bodies placed in it—the victims of the Vigilantes having been buried in a field apart from the others. When I first visited the site of old Hell Gate and for a good many years after, there were mounds visible where the burials had been made. But time has worn these level and there is nothing left to show that the scythe slashed vigorously for a little while in the days when Hell Gate died with its boots on.

October 1911

71

Notes:

Hell's Gate Canyon was named by the French Trappers who visited the area in the early 1800's. Numerous raids on other tribes by the Blackfeet Tribe in the natural bottleneck of the canyon had left the area littered with bones. Horrified at this evidence of carnage, trappers called the canyon "Porte de l'Enfer" or the "Gates of Hell".

Hellgate Village or Ronde - There is nothing left of Hellgate Village now. St. Michael's Church, built by Father Grassi, is the only surviving building from Hellgate. After spending several years on the St. Patrick Hospital campus, it was moved to Fort Missoula where it is to this day. The original setting of Hellgate was four miles from Missoula on Mullan Road.

The Virginia City Vigilantes were formed in 1863 after about 100 people were killed in "road agent" robberies earlier in the year. Locals soon became convinced that the road agents were all one group led by Bannack Sheriff Henry Plummer. Over the course of six weeks, the vigilantes executed 21 road agents including the men in Hellgate. In the summer of 1864, territorial law was established in Montana which deemed the acts of vigilantes to be criminal.

The Coriacan Defile is three miles north of Evaro, MT off of US Route 93. Its name comes from a Kanaka Indian named Koriaka. He was shot and killed by a Blackfeet war party as he led a Hudson's Bay brigade into the valley next to where the Marent's Trestle is now located.

HOW JUDGE WOODY MET A BOLD BANDIT

True Story of Encounter with Plummer in Pioneer
Days---Rascal Was a
Courteous and Entertaining Chap to Meet

I am probably the first white man who saw Henry Plummer, the road agent, when he first entered what is now the state of Montana. In 1860 Worden & Company established a store and trading post about four miles below the present city of Missoula. I was employed as a clerk in their store from the time it was established until the spring of 1862, when I quit their employment and went and located at Gold Creek, then in the county of Powell. In the spring of 1862, some parties commenced placer mining in Pioneer Gulch, a tributary of Gold Creek, and quite a number of men were employed there. At a point on Gold Creek near its mouth, a little hamlet grew up, consisting of two stores, two saloons and a few dwellings. This hamlet was called Gold Creek or American Fork and was the supply point for the miners and was a place of gathering of the miners, travelers and the few settlers in that section of the country. I was stopping at this place and so were the Stuart brothers, James and Granville.

Some time in the latter part of August or early part of September, 1862, Granville Stuart and I saddled our horses and rode down the Hell Gate canyon to Worden and company's store at Hell Gate, and, having no place to stop except the store, we made our headquarters with Captain Higgins there. He had an old French lady named Mrs. Pelky as cook, and kept a small mess house for his own use and for the use of such visitors and wayfarers as might stop there. After we had been there two or three days, Captain Higgins said to me that he wanted to take a little ride and asked me if I would take care of the store for him while he was gone. I told him I would. Soon thereafter, Granville Stuart saddled up his horse and started on a ride. I was left at the store alone. About 2 or 3 o'clock in the afternoon two men rode up to the store on horseback with a double-barreled shotgun and a revolver. They had their roll of blankets tied on behind their saddles. Their horses appeared to be nearly worn out with travel. They came into the store and asked me if there was any chance to get something to eat. I told them we would not have dinner until about 6 o'clock, but that we had an old lady cook who probably could give them a little lunch. I went out and saw the old lady and she said she would get them something to eat. I came back to the store and they asked me if there was any show to get a drink of whiskey and said they needed a drink very much. I told them there was none there to sell, that the proprietor of the store was absent, but he had a small quantity for his own use and probably I could get them a drink. I found Captain Higgin's keg and poured them out enough whiskey to give each one of them a good drink. Then they went and had their lunch and came back to the store and spent the afternoon with me.

There was nothing singular in their appearance. One of them was a man probably 35 years old and the other a young man about 20 or 21. The eldest man told me his name was Henry Plummer and the young man was Charley Reeves. Then they went on to explain their appearance there and said that they had been over in a mining camp on the west side of the Bitter Root mountains, called Oro Fino, which at that time was quite a lively mining camp, having several saloons, dance halls, etc., and quite a crowd of men in the camp. They said that few days before they were in a dance hall and got into a quarrel with the proprietor of the place, named O'Neil or McNeil, I do not remember which and the difficulty resulted in a fight and shooting, and they were compelled to kill the proprietor, O'Neil or McNeil, who was an Irishman; that the camp was full of Irishmen and from what they saw and heard of threats being made they were satisfied that if they did not get out of there that the Irish would mob them and probably kill them.

They gathered their belongings, consisting of blanket and arms, saddled their horses and struck across the mountains for the Bitter Root, finally coming over the Lolo Fork trail and when they came out of the canyon they found a road or trail and, following that, it brought them to Worden and company's store at Hell Gate. They stayed at the store for one or two days, then rode over to the Flathead agency on the Jocko and remained there a day or two, and came back. They evidently were undecided as to where they would go, but when Mr. Stuart and I told them we were stopping at Gold Creek and that a new mining camp was just starting, they concluded to go with us up there.

When they came back from the agency, Reeve's horse was too lame to travel farther and, as I was going up the next day with four or five horses. I told Reeves he could leave his horse with Worden and company and ride one of mine up to Gold Creek. With which offer he was very much pleased. The next day we got ready to start, put a pack saddle on one horse and blankets on and coffee pot and frying pan, and were off late in the day up the canyon. That evening we arrived at that creek that comes down from the mountains where Bonita now is and was called at that time Beaver Tail Creek or some called it Beaver Dam Creek. We camped there and left our horses with the cook and ate supper, went to bed, and slept soundly, with the two road agents, without knowing that they were such. In the morning, after getting our breakfast we started and arrived at Gold Creek late in the afternoon.

That man Plummer and also Reeves were fairly well dressed and did not look like laboring men, but I had no suspicion as to their being road agents. Reeves acknowledged that he was a gambler, and after they had been at Gold Creek a few days there was more or less gambling going on and Reeves was generally into any game that was started. After being there a few days, they went over the Sun Creek trail to the Indian agency. What their idea was in going there, I never knew. After remaining for some time, they came back and in the meantime Grasshopper Creek mines had been struck and the little town of Bannock had commenced to grow. They came there without any sensible business, but Reeves engaged in gambling.

Plummer was one of the most polite men I have ever known---a regular Chesterfield in politeness; a man of good appearance and the last man that one would take to be a highwayman. He drank very little, was very sociable and good company. After I had furnished them horses to ride from Hell Gate to Deer Lodge. Plummer took quite a liking to me and was willing to do any favor I might ask and never dreamed or imagined that he was a road agent, until after I learned he had been hanged as such.

His life and history in Montana are too well known to the history of the state to need retelling.

Frank H. Woody
December 1914

Notes:

"Chesterfield in politeness" refers to a book written by Lord Chesterfield in 1786 called *Principles of Politeness, and of Knowing the World.*

Road Agents were bandits that robbed travelers especially those traveling in stagecoaches.

OLD TIMER'S YARNS

STORIES TOLD OF THE EARLY PIONEER DAYS

———

Many and varied were the stories told by the old timers of Montana, who were recently congregated in this city. Among the numerous anecdotes told were the following:

"Frank," said J. Chatfield to Judge Frank H. Woody of Missoula county, "I think I know that man."

"You ought to," was the reply.

This conversation took place at Hamilton on the occasion of the Pioneers' excursion to that place last week from Missoula where the old-timers had met in annual reunion.

Mr. Chatfield had been introduced to the pioneer by Judge Woody and the two had walked away after the introduction.

"I should think you would," repeated the judge. "and I will recall him to you. You saw him but once to my knowledge and then under what is now called strenuous circumstances. Do you remember being in Worden & Co.'s store at Hell Gate one cold night in December, 1863?"

"Very well, I now know the man."

"I thought you would."

"That was a warm night," the judge continued. "A party of us were seated in the store, playing cards. Several others were lounging about in chairs or on the counter. Worden's store was the general rendezvous for all traveling through the valley. There were fully a dozen in the store. One man was keeping the stove red hot. Besides our party playing cards at one table there were four others seated at another table, playing. Suddenly I heard someone say, 'I can shoot as well as ye.' Looking up I saw three men on their feet, all with revolvers drawn. One of the men was the man who had been attending to the fire. He was a stranger who had recently come into the valley and had been given room to spread his blankets. The other two were men who had been playing cards.

"The shooting commenced. There was a scatter of us all. I hugged the floor and I suppose everybody else did. The lights went out or were shot out, but the shooting went on in the dark. Besides the popping we could hear men struggling and breathing hard. Then, all at once, silence. When we ventured to light up, one man was lying dead upon the floor, another was sitting in a chair desperately wounded, and the third man had disappeared. The wounded man recovered. We buried the dead man. I did not see the man who disappeared for twenty years. There was never any attempt made to arrest him. He is now an honored member of society and one of the best men living. He is the man Chatfield recognized. We frequently meet, but neither has ever spoken of that night at Hell Gate. I don't know who was in the right or the wrong. I only know that when bullets are flying thick and fast in a room that I am in, I can make a floor sag in my efforts to press down into the basement. His name? I don't know what his name was in the states."

October 1901

"TOO MANY BEARS"

This Bear Story Sounds Romantic, but it
Must Be True, Because It Was Written by a
Montana District Judge.

During the winter of 1862 and 1863 quite a
number of men, of whom the writer was one, wintered
on the flat opposite the mouth of the Gallatin river, and
built a large number of houses---in fact laid out and built
a town and called it "Three Forks" and all were wealthy
in expectation, as each member of the community was
possessed in his own right of any number of corner lots.
In the spring of 1863, no steamboats having signified
their intention of coming up the Missouri to our landing,
the demand for the purchase of corner lots was not as
great as many of us had anticipated, and there being no
sale for the wood that we had cut and corded up during
the winter, with which to burn brick in the spring to
meet the anticipated demand of the building boom that
we all felt certain would occur, several of us began
casting about to find some chance to get out and get a
square meal.

A party of seven or eight of us, among whom I
remember William Tracey, now of Bozeman, Major
William Grahame, and a man and his wife named
Roush, afterwards of Bozeman, with three or four
wagons and ox teams, conceived the brilliant idea of

80

opening a new road from the Three Forks to Benton---
Fort Benton then called---going down on the east side of
the Missouri river, through a country, concerning which
none of us knew anything whatever. We crossed the
Jefferson and Gallatin rivers just above the confluence,
crossed over some cedar covered hills and down into the
Missouri river, and followed down the river, passing the
place where Townsend is now situated, keeping in near
the foothills, passing down by and near what was
afterwards Confederate gulch and on till we struck a
large Indian trail that we afterwards learned was call the
Flathead Indian trail left the Missouri valley and
followed up a small creek, which I have since learned
was afterwards called White's gulch.

Leaving this gulch we followed the trail up the
mountain side and after some hard work succeeded in
landing our wagons on top, where the country opened
out into a somewhat broken, partly prairie and partly
timbered country, where we had a splendid camp. The
Indian trail bearing too much to the east, we concluded
to abandon it, and turned north, traveling as we
supposed, parallel with the Missouri river. Being
somewhat short of meat I took my saddle horse and gun,
a muzzle loading rifle, and rode on in advance to try and
kill some game. I had a navy revolver and only a few
matches. I took nothing with me to eat, expecting to be
with the wagons again in a few hours. I had with me a
young black and tan fox-hound, with no more sense
than the traditional hound pup.

We had no definite understanding as to our route,
and were simply feeling our way through the country. I
rode on in the direction that I supposed the wagons
would take, and after going a few miles, saw an
antelope, and fooled away some time trying to get a shot
at it, but was not successful in so doing, and first thing

that I knew it was about 10 o'clock, and I had secured no game, nor were there any wagons in sight. This was about the middle of May, the weather clear and pleasant, the hills covered with green grass and flowers, and feeling in a pleasant frame of mind, the absence of the wagons did not in the least disturb me, as I felt certain that I was in the only open country through which they could pass. I concluded to ride on and see if I could find some game, and riding up the slope of a hill I saw about one hundred yards to my right a bear lying down in a shallow wash or gully. He had not discovered me and was evidently sleeping.

As I was not particularly hunting bears that day and being in an exceedingly good humor, and not looking for any trouble, I concluded that I would not disturb him, which I proceeded to do, keeping away from him about 125 yards. I had gotten on the other side of him, and about 100 yards from him, and was riding along slowly and keeping a watch on him and admiring his immense size---he was a large grizzly---when my horse struck his foot against a stone, making a noise that awakened the bear from a sound slumber. He raised himself up on his haunches, and gazed at me much like a drunken man, presenting too tempting a mark for me to resist, though well knowing the danger. The dog had not yet seen him. My horse was none too gentle, but I jumped off and kneeling down Indian fashion, I aimed at his breast, and at the crack of the gun he went over on his back, and I went onto my horse. Bruin scrambled about for a minute or so, recovered his feet and made for a deep wooded hollow a few hundred yards off, with the dog after him, but I did not follow.

The dog returned safe and sound in a short time. There was no danger of him getting hurt, as he had more discretion than any other dog that I ever saw. I then rode on up the slope to the top, and looking over what appeared to have been the rim of a small lake at some time, I saw quite a large basin, say 300 or 400 acres, bounded on the east side about half way round with a ridge or rim covered with large granite boulders. In the basin I saw as I sat on my horse seven bears busily engaged in digging some kind of roots. Nearly all of them appeared to be immense fellows, either brown or grizzlies. I made up my mind that I would make no trouble, though I was after meat. After surveying the field over I noticed four of them off quite a distance in a brush and near the rim or rocky side bounding the flat or swale on the east, and I at once concluded that three of them looked small and black, and I fancied I had found some black bear. I had often been told by hunters that the black bear was not dangerous, and that their meat was good, so I immediately made up my mind that I would take some bear meat back to the wagons for I had no doubt but what I would find my companions in camp without any trouble. How well I succeeded as a bear hunter the reader will soon learn.

I thought to ride around, keeping behind the rim or ridge and out of sight until I could come to a point opposite the place where I had seen the four bears, thinking that I would then be near enough to get a shot at one of them. I rode on, keeping well behind the rocky rim until I thought that I was about the right place. I then dismounted, taking the rope, which was tied around the horse's neck, and usually tied to the horn of the saddle, in my hand, and leading the horse, the dog following, and approached the rim of the depression, keeping well behind a huge boulder, that was about as high as my shoulder. When I had reached the rock, I dropped the rope on the ground and raised myself up so I could see what had become of my game. As I looked over the rock, I was surprised to see my four bears about 100 yards distant coming towards me on a big lope, and what was still worse, I discovered that they were not blacks at all, but four grizzlies, one old one and three yearlings.

This was, I thought, taking an undue advantage of me, and made me feel decidedly embarrassed. I stand and looked at them a few seconds, and then remembered that old hunters had told me that bear would not voluntarily attack a man if let alone, so I did not feel much alarmed. They had evidently seen the top of my head while I was on my horse, and their curiosity being excited, they were bent on finding out what it was, and what it all meant. Not seriously apprehending any danger I stepped out from behind the rock in plain view, they were then about 40 yards distant, and just at this moment the fool dog for the first time discovered them, and did just what no dog but a fool hound pup would have done. Just as soon as he saw them he raised his bristles and all of his hair standing straight out, he made a deliberate charge towards them. The old bear threw open her mouth and charged straight for the dog with the yearlings right at her flank, the froth flying from the old one's mouth, while she gnashed her teeth and went for the dog. The horse was standing just behind me.

The dog made straight for me with all four bears after him. As the horse saw the dog and bears coming he jerked the rope from under my foot, where I had put it to hold him, and took to his heels and ran as he had never ran before, with the dog a close second, leaving me to receive the brunt of the charge. The reader may laugh and think that this is exceedingly funny, but just at that time I failed to see where the fun came in. When the horse and dog left me I began to think over my past life, and also what I was to do. I doubt if ever a man thought as much in the same length of time as I did then. The bears came up to within about 20 feet, when they apparently saw me for the first time. They came to a full stop and glared at me, the old one with her mouth open and her jaws covered with froth. She looked to be as large as an ox and the young ones did not look small. I suppose that I glared at her. I had my gun cocked and to my shoulder, but I knew that it was death if I fired and did not kill her, and I could have no reasonable hope of doing that. It is true I had my revolver, but I also knew that it would be of but little if any use. In about a half a second I made up my mind what to do. It was to keep a bead on her eye, but not to fire unless she started to advance, in which case I had made up my mind to give her the best reception that I was able to, though I had but little doubt how it would terminate. We all stood perfectly still, and eyed one another for probably five seconds, though to me it seemed a lifetime, when she gave me a snort and turned and ran as I never had seen a bear run before, with the young ones at her heels. Up to this time my muscles had been almost rigid, but the moment that she turned and ran they relaxed and I became so weak that I had to lean against the large rock for support, while the perspiration stood out on my forehead in great drops. I watched the bears and made sure they were gone, then followed up my horse and dog, caught the horse and mounted, feeling decidedly thankful that the old bear had changed her mind and had concluded to confine herself to her usual diet of roots. It was now about noon, with no bear meat, nor wagons in sight, and worst of all, I did not know where they were or which way to go, for whichever way I would go I would see bears, but I had had enough of them for one day. On this day I saw and counted 14 different bears. There were acres of ground dug up, which had been dug by the bears for roots. There was a small ground vine that looked something like cinquefoil, the root of which they soon found. This section of the country was some high rolling country between the Bear Tooth mountains and the Smith river.

To continue, I rode on until in the afternoon, when I reached a small fine valley, where I rested myself and horse, and while resting I saw an elk come down off of the hills and enter a clump of willows some half mile off. I made a still hunt and killed the elk. I cut off what I could well carry on my horse and ride, and started for what I took to be a low piece of country, and through which I felt the wagons must pass, but the fact was I was in a strange country, and had become lost. I rode on till after sunset, and had reached some timber and the head of a ravine, which I followed until it became too dark to travel. I then unsaddled and tied my horse to a tree, took my saddle blanket and made me a bed and went to sleep, having had nothing to eat since early in the morning.

In the morning I arose early, saddled my horse, threw away my elk meat except a few pounds, started down the ravine again, and after going probably half a mile I came to quite a good sized creek. Here I grazed my horse, built a fire and cooking some of my meat I had a first class breakfast. I found that I was in a deep canon, with no visible way of getting out, so I rode down the stream, satisfied that it must lead to the Missouri, but not knowing if I could follow down the canon. However I kept going, sometimes on a gravel bar and sometimes in the water, with the walls of the canon so high that I could not always see out. I continued on down the stream until late in the afternoon when I came out of the canon into the open prairie, and I could see the Missouri in the distance. Here I rested a short time and starting a fire with my last match and cooked some more meat and took dinner.

I then rode on till near sunset and reached the mouth of the stream where it joined the Missouri. At this point there was an Indian trail, but no sign of any wagons and I then knew that they must be behind me, for there was no possible show for them to have passed to the east of me, judging from the looks of the country. Here at the mouth of this creek I made another camp and passed the night. During the night it commenced to rain and my saddle blanket was not much protection, and in the morning I was soaking wet. During the night I could hear the falls roaring and then I knew about where I was. My meat was used up, and so was my matches. I saddled up and started early, keeping well back from the river to avoid the deep lateral coulies, which were difficult to cross. During the day I killed an antelope and took some of the meat and on reaching a small stream where there was a little timber I tried to make a fire with my gun, but everything was so wet that I failed.

About this time I began to feel like eating something, but I rode on and reached the river bank opposite Fort Benton just before sunset, fired off my gun, and a man came over with a skiff and took me over. Here I found some Bannack and also Missoula friends, and was then all O. K. I learned there that the stream that I had followed down was Deep creek, now called Smith River.

My party with the wagons did not get into Fort Benton until seven days after my arrival. That trip gave me enough of bear hunting, and I have had no desire to repeat it. I made two more trips over nearly the same ground the same summer and fall and in passing over these rolling hills never saw less than nine bears in one day, and in a distance of some five or six miles. It was the greatest country for bears that I ever saw or heard of.

FRANK H. WOODY
December 1897

Notes:

Three Forks is so named because it is located at the confluence of three rivers, the Jefferson, the Gallatin, and the Madison, forming the headwaters of the Missouri River.

First Montana Steamboats

About the time of the launching of the "City of Dixon," the little river steamer which was built at Dixon to navigate the Flathead river and give the people along its course a much needed passenger and freight service, the statement was made that it was the first boat of its kind ever constructed in western Montana. Judge F.H. Woody took exceptions to this statement and in discussing the matter said that he remembered well the time when three boats were operated on the Clark's Fork river from Lake Pend d'Orielle into Montana as far as the Cabinet gorge. Two of these, as he remembered, were built on the lake but the other one, the "Missoula" was constructed on this side of the line and did good service. "I can't remember all of the circumstances," said Judge Woody, "but back in 1866 or '67 I wrote an article on early modes of transportation on western Montana for the Historical Society of Montana. It was published and I have the volume in which it appears. I did not mention anything about where the 'Missoula' was built; that part of the story I remember well enough. But the other facts are all accurate for they were set down when the information was all fresh in mind." The judge then turned to the page where the article referred to appears and read the following section:

"In the spring and summer of 1865 rich and extensive gold mines were found on Little Blackfoot river and its tributaries, and also on the tributaries of the Big Blackfoot river in Deer Lodge county that induced an immense immigration from California and Oregon and from the territories of Idaho and Washington.

Nearly all of the vast crowd of gold seekers came over the Coeur d'Alene mountains by way of the wagon road constructed by Lieutenant John Mullan, and passed through the Hell's Gate Ronde. During the whole of the summer and fall of 1865 the road was literally lined with men and animals on their way to the new El Dorado. At this time a large portion of the supplies used in the mining camps of Montana, were purchased in San Francisco and Portland and were transported from Walla Walla, Washington Territory, on pack mules over the Coeur d'Alene mountains by way of Hell's Gate and Missoula to the various mining camps of Montana. So great was this trade that hundreds and even thousands of pack mules were employed in this business and times were unusually lively in western Montana. It was during the summer of 1865 that some parties brought up, by this same route from Nevada or Idaho, a number of camels loaded with merchandise. These were the first, and I believe the only camels ever brought to Montana for such a purpose, and were a source of wonder and surprise to the Indians, who had never before seen anything like them. The adventure did not prove a success to the parties engaged in it. One of the camels died at the Mullan crossing of the Missoula river below Missoula; another was shot and killed near Blackfoot city by a hunter who had never seen a camel and who thought it was a moose. The same lot of camels are now doing duty in Arizona packing merchandise from Yuma City into the interior.

"It being impossible to cross the Coeur d'Alene mountains earlier than the month of July, the spring travel came up by Pend d'Oreille lake and Clark's fork of the Columbia. The vast amount of travel over this route each spring, together with the expectation that the Northern Pacific railroad would speedily be completed

90

and would pass down Clark's Fork, induced the Oregon Steam Navigation company of Portland to put a line of steamboats on the lake and river for the purpose of shortening the land transportation to Montana. The company commenced operations in the fall of 1865 and in four months from the time the first tree was felled for her, a steamboat was launched and floated on the bosom of the lake. She was 108 feet in length, 20 feet beam and was 85 tons burden, constructed entirely of whip-sawed lumber. This boat was built on the western shore of the lake in Idaho territory. She was christened the 'Mary Moody' and made her first trip in the spring of 1866, coming across the lake and up Clark's Fork about 15 miles to the Cabinet landing, just outside Montana. This was the first steamboat that ever navigated the waters of western Montana. The following winter the company constructed two more boats to ply on Clark's Fork above the Cabinet mountains. One of these, the 'Cabinet' ran from the upper end of the Cabinet falls to the rapids at Rock Island, and the other the 'Missoula', ran from the upper end of the Rock Island rapids to Thompson's Falls. These boats did a good business for two or three years, but after that time, the travel having fallen off, the boats were, in the summer of 1870, run down over the falls to the lower or western end of the lake, where the machinery was taken out and conveyed to the lower Columbia river. That the reader may form some idea of the vast travel through this portion of Montana from 1865 to 1870, I will state that the year 1869 was an unusually dull year owing to the lack of water in the mining camps, but during that year the steamboat company reported that they conveyed on their boats about 4,000 animals and their packs, and that many packers passed with their trains around the northern end of the lake by a trail difficult to pass in wet seasons.

The Camels

"How about those camels?" Judge Woody was asked.

"Well, sir, that was a queer thing," he said. "It was during Buchanan's administration, I think, that a committee was appointed by the government to go to Asia and purchase a bunch of camels and bring them back to use in transporting government stores and supplies for the soldiers stationed at posts in Texas. When the war broke out and the southern posts were abandoned, the camels were turned loose. They were later rounded up by some enterprising citizens and brought to Arizona, and later several trips were made with them into Montana. This was about '65, and that winter the camels were taken to Blackfoot City, then a thriving little mining town on the Little Blackfoot river, and turned loose on the range for the winter. Then a funny thing happened. There was a little Irishman there who was quite a hunter. One day he came tearing into camp, all excited, and told the story of having found a bank of elk, one of which he shot. 'Come on, byes,' he cried. 'Ther's a hell of a fine bunch of elk out there, and wel'll get the whole dom works.' That Irishman had shot a camel, and it cost him $700 or $800 before he got through with the case.

In this climate, some of them died. "But the camels didn't do very well that winter, and the rest were taken back to Arizona. I have heard that some of them are still in existence, but was never able to verify this report."

December 15th, 1912

Misquoted

"You've made me out the biggest liar in 47 states," said Judge Woody to a Missoulian reporter yesterday. "In that story about the camels in the Holiday Missoulian you quote me as saying that the beasts were brought to the Blackfoot country to winter. Now, any fool would know better than that, for a camel is not built for hard winters, such as we used to have in the Blackfoot. It was summer time when the camels were turned loose to rest a few days after having been packed in with supplies. You had the rest of the story all right, but I don't want anyone to think that I said the camels were brought here to be wintered."

December 17th, 1912

Note:

The City of Dixon Steamboat was launched in September 1912. It ran from Dixon, MT to Sloan's Ferry west of Ronan, MT. In August of 1914 it was struck by lightning and burned down. It wasn't replaced.

YE OLDEN TIME SYSTEM

The Way Income Taxes Were Collected in Early Days Here

JUDGE WOODY TELLS A TALE

His Salary in Greenbacks Was Small, But the Amount He Paid for Drawing it Was Big---Gold for Paper Money

Local bondholders and corporations have filled out and sent in the inquisitorial blanks which are necessary in making returns for the levying of the income tax and this probably is the first time that any of them wished that the income of the business represented were less than it is. There is some consolation in being poor, even if there are discomforts incident to poverty, and the fact that a poor man is not liable to the income tax payment is one of the advantages of a scanty purse. It is not known just how much Missoula will contribute toward making good Mr. Carlisle's deficit but the amount will indicate that this is a fairly prosperous community, despite the hard times.

In speaking of the income tax to a Standard reporter the other day, Judge Woody remarked, "I believe that I am the only man in Montana who has ever paid an income tax. But I paid one once and paid a big one, much bigger than it ought to have been. I have made some inquiry and have never discovered anybody else who fell a victim to the rapacious greed of the revenue collectors who operated in this section during war time, which was the time that I was forced to contribute to the national treasury by paying a tax upon my meager income."

Upon being asked to tell the story, Judge Woody continued as follows: "It was in the spring of 1865 and I was in the employ of Worden & Co. as clerk in their store at the old town of Hell Gate, down the river. I was at work in the store one day, when an internal revenue collector entered and, without beating about the bush at all, informed me that he had come to assess my income of the previous year. During the last three years of the war we people of Montana had come to have a very wholesome respect for the revenue collectors and the United States marshals, as we were absolutely in their power, and our courts were in such a crude condition that redress was impossible to obtain without the loss of considerable time and money. When these fellows saw a good thing and were in need of a little money, they went after it, and all that a man could do was to obey them. There are numerous instances of gross wrongs perpetrated by those government officers and more than one innocent and honest man was made to suffer to satisfy them.

"Consequently, I was somewhat alarmed when this collector, whose name was Romulus C. Percy, said 'I want to assess you for your income of last year.' I put on a bold front and replied that there wasn't much to assess, as my income was pretty small.

"'How much did you get a month last year,' was his next question. He was evidently determined to form his own opinion of the size of my income.

"I replied, 'My wages are $75 a month, but I worked only 10 months last year.'

"'That makes $750 for the year?' said the collector, and I agreed that his reckoning was correct.

"At that time $600 was exempt in computing the income tax and the remainder was levied upon at the rate of five per cent. I thought that, even if I was compelled to pay a tax it would be small, as five per cent of $150 was not very much. At that time, greenbacks were worth out here only 33 1/3 cents on the dollar and there were but a few of them to be obtained anyway. This rascally collector took advantage of that fact and when he asked his next question I knew that I was done for.

"'What have you been getting your pay in?' was the query.

"'In gold dust,' I answered.

"'At what rate?'

"'Eighteen dollars an ounce.'

"Then the villain sat down and figured out my wages in greenbacks at 33 1/3 cents on the dollar and calmly informed me that my income was really $2,250 and I would have to pay tax on that sum less $600. This brought it down to $1,650 and, figuring 5 per cent. of that, the smooth rascal told me without a quiver, that he would let me off with $82.50."

"I argued with him and pleaded with him, but without making any impression upon him and I finally saw that it was no use and told him that I would pay it. Then I tried to find some greenbacks to pay him with, but there was not one in town and, after a vain search, I said, 'I will have to pay in gold dust.'

"'All right.' Was the reply.

"I then proceeded to convert the gold dust into greenback value and was planning to pay him $27.50 on the same basis that he had assessed my income. He wouldn't have it that way at all. He could estimate my income in greenbacks, but I must pay a dollar in dust for a dollar in greenbacks. That was the decision of Romulus C. Percy and from that decision there was no appeal. I was obliged to weigh out $82.50 in clean American gold dust. And that is the way I paid income tax, $82.50 on an income of $750.

"I doubt very much if the national treasury ever saw any of this money, but if it did, it is safe to say that it was in greenbacks and that Romulus C. Percy put $55 into his inside pocket. But I fared much easier than did some of the residents of this section who were pounced upon by the United States marshals on trumped-up charges. More than one man was made penniless by their extortions."

April 1895

Note:

Mr. Carlisle's deficit refers to John G. Carlisle who was Secretary of the Treasury of the United States from 1893 to 1897. His political career was ruined by the Panic of 1893, a serious financial and economic depression. He ended up leaving political life in 1897.

Pretty Bill from Yam Hill

————

"He never worked and he never will"

That is the way Frank H. Woody (now Judge Woody) introduced William C. Darnold to Mrs. Jim Buckley at a dance in Missoula in the fall of 1866. Jim Buckley was sheriff. He and Woody didn't care much about dances; they wanted to play a game of croquet and Woody volunteered to find an escort for Mrs. Buckley. So he picked out Darnold, a tenderfoot kid then, and took him around to the lady. When it came to the introduction, Woody couldn't remember Darnold's name, so he invented the "Pretty Bill." And as long as he lived in Missoula Darnold was called "Pretty Bill" after that. Mr. Darnold, now a resident of Bremerton Wash., has been making Missoula a visit. He returned to the coast yesterday morning. While he was here he called upon a few of his friends, but his time here was so short that he had not time to see them all. He left a greeting for all of them, however, and asked the Man About Town to deliver it for him. "I struck Missoula July 20, 1866, said Mr. Darnold, in telling his early experiences here. "I had come up from Blackfoot with a bull team and I was glad to get to even the small town that Missoula was then. There were not very many people here then. I recall the men I learned to like as friends that summer. I was a kid of eighteen then and they were good to me. There was Frank Woody, of course; everybody in town knew him then, just as now. The list is not long; there were Frank Worden, Captain Higgins, Charles Hayden, A. Harding, Ned Bonner, Dan Welch, John Hall and Jim Buckley – I think that is pretty nearly the roll call of the whole voting list at that time. But it was a fine lot of men and they made things as pleasant for me as they could. I was never sorry that I came to Missoula, even though Woody did stick that "Pretty Bill" name on to me. I stayed in Missoula until 1872. Then I went away for a while and came back. Now I am located on the coast. Four years ago I came back here with the body of my wife, who was a sister of Mrs. Frank Worden and who had died on the coast. I had not been here since until now. I wish I could stay long enough to see all of my old friends, but I have to hurry back and I wish you would just let them know I have been here and left my regards for each one of them."

April 1913

FORTY YEARS AGO REMEMBERED – "DANCEHALLS"

MR. AND MRS. T.R. DANA, PIONEER RESIDENTS, GUESTS AT WOODY HOME

"A chiel's amang ye, takin' notes." At first it was all too evident, but when the recollections and stories started they fairly reeled off the tongues of the two modest people who are visiting Judge and Mrs. Woody. Sitting in the cozy, up-to-date library of the Woody home, surrounded by every evidence of the 20th century, the minds traveled a long road back to that turn of their life road where the mile stone pointed the way to Missoula for Mr. and Mrs. T.T. Dana, now of Slack, Wyo. and formerly one of 'em right here. But it was Judge Woody who must have been the "broth of a boy" by all accounts, of his own and of his friends.

Mrs. Dana was, perhaps, along back in the '70s, as popular as any woman who ever found her home west. By that token, she is greeted everywhere by her old friends with the greatest affection. Her dark eyes are sweet and earnest yet, if not quite so brilliant as formerly. Her husband is really apple-cheeked, and this couple, wending its way together down the hill of life, is a pleasant spectacle. It was Judge Woody who started to speak of the dance clubs which flourished here in the 70's or thereabouts. A good sized carpenter shop stood on the site of the Florence hotel and the dancers used to sweep the shavings and sawdust back in the shop and then dance till 5 in the morning.

"I don't know, how I ever stood it, either," said Mrs. Dana. "But I recollect going three consecutive nights and dancing till 5! Two of these events I had Mr. Dana with me; the third he positively refused to budge from the house, so I went with friends." She laughed delightfully at the memory.

"But, oh, then when we had the then new courthouse," she continued, "we used to dance in the courtroom. I went up there yesterday, but it has been partitioned off into anterooms, I don't like it," and she shook her head pensively.

"The dancing clubs were 'The Silk Stocking club' and 'The Gum Shoe club' and while there were plenty of gum shoes in evidence I don't suppose there was a silk stocking in town," put in Mrs. Woody and we all laughed appreciatively.

There was an orchestra, too, in town and when it could do so without too much trouble it played for the dances. Three pieces usually furnished music and Jacob and James Reinhardt and, maybe, Ferd Kennett, belonged to it. A man from the eastern part of the state was engaged as instructor at $150 a month. The instruments were brought from St. Louis. Of one of the musical geniuses it is recorded that he was once jilted or near-jilted and that he, for some time after, perched on a fence in the moonlight and practiced dolefully and untunefully alone.

The only uptown landmark remaining to the recollection of the visitors is the little sandwich, now occupied by a fruit stand, between the Leiser block and the Missoula hotel. This had stood on West Front street and was built by A. W. Ross and Dr. Heinke had it as a drugstore. Afterward, it was moved to West Main street and W. H. H. Dickinson occupied it when he was postmaster. The old Rodgers house had formerly been the Dana house, and the Cottage hotel, on the site of what is now the Rankin hotel, was also kept by the Danas. It was here, if the date is not mixed too much, that Washington J. McCormick and Miss Kate Higgins were married. At any rate, they lived with the Danas for some time after they were married, in 1869. Judge Woody had been called away in a great hurry to see Louis Brown of Frenchtown, who, believing himself to be dying, sent also for Father Ravalli. Securing a buckboard, the Judge lost not a minute, but drove on the jump to "eighteen miles be-low," arriving covered in mud and slush. The patient was found sitting on the side of the bed smoking a short black pipe. The will was made and two weeks later Louis Brown headed the stampede into---was it Cedar Creek? Into somewhere, at all events. Returning to town, Judge Woody found the entire male population hugely enjoying itself, celebrating the wedding with a glorious charivari. The groom refused to "stake" the crowd and it is a fact that for almost a whole week the attention was showered upon the hotel till Mr. Dana told the groom to stop it or leave the house. He had never lost so much sleep in his life.

The newspapers received a word also. Prior to even the "Pioneer" print, was a paper called the "Missoula and Cedar Creek Journal" and a printer named Morrison ran off the first issue on a hand press, in 1869. The first paper off the press was presented to the wife of this printer. Judge Woody secured the second and says he is sure it has been preserved. He wrestled with his seldom-failing memory for the name of a printer who once worked there who was a character. The "Missoula and Cedar Creek Journal" gave place to the "Pioneer" and later Judge Woody took the fortunes of the publication over and called it the "Missoulian." There is some difference between this journal of so many years ago, which furnished news to the 200 or so people of this town, and this morning's Missoulian, which goes out to so many homes (for accurate information see our circulator).

Of the many stories and the almost pathetic eagerness of recollecting the lively past, there can only be said that it has been a season of complete happiness for many people in Missoula to meet again Mr. and Mrs. Dana, whose visit is to be concluded all too soon. The pity grows upon us that, if someone is not active before long, all this rich material lying to one's hand will be lost. The pioneer history of Missoula is not by any means all in the history of Montana. There is a history of pioneer women which would mean much if brought to completion.

And Judge Woody, for once, has failed. He can't remember who was that printer.

March 1910

Notes:

"A Chiel's amang ye" is a Scottish term indicating a bloke or chap is in your midst.

Charivari or a shivaree is a mock serenade (usually noisy and discordant) held at the residence of a newly wed couple. The revelers will sometimes hold out for a bribe from the groom to stop their clamoring. It appears that Mr. McCormick wouldn't pay them a "stake", so they kept coming back night after night.

TO THE BISHOP'S CREDIT

Some Stories of Early Days in Missoula

A CRACKERJACK VESTRY

A Promising Set of Notables Who Never Attended Church---The Story of a Gun and a Watch---It Was a Tough Game

The presence of Bishop Tuttle in Missoula has recalled to the old-timers many of the incidents of the days when his diocese included Missoula and when he was laboring to maintain a church in this town, then a small settlement. It is needless to say that all of these stories that are being told are much to the credit of the bishop and serve to indicate that the Missoula church was not the banner parish, by any means, of the jurisdiction over which the bishop presided. Bishop Tuttle's chief trouble seems to have been with the vestrymen. They were good citizens and realized the necessity of having a church in the city. They were willing to and did contribute in the maintenance of the church, but they were too busy and had been too long in the wilderness to fall easily into the practice of strengthening the infant parish by their presence at services. One set of vestrymen after another was tried and each was a little bit worse than the one that had preceded it. From all accounts, the banner vestry was the one that was composed of Judge Frank H. Woody, Frank L. Worden, G. A. Wolf and Henry McFarlane. It is not altogether easy at this remote distance to believe that these men ever served on a church board, but the records are indisputable. They were regularly appointed by the bishop at the time of one of his visits here and they served their term some of them held over for other terms, too.

The story goes that the bishop returned to Missoula after an absence of a year or more, after he secured this promising vestry, and, after the services had been held and the bishop had talked things over and looked about somewhat, he called a meeting of the vestrymen. All hands turned out and the meeting was held in the office of Mr. Wolf. The bishop spoke pleasantly of the progress that the church had made and then brought up some matters to which his attention had been called during his visit. They were questions of importance that pertained directly to the church and its work. He asked the opinion of the vestrymen at first collectively, and then, when no response was elicited, individually. All of the vestrymen and then each of the vestrymen looked solemn and said nothing. The bishop persisted in his question and Mr. Worden said, "Well, bishop, we might as well tell the truth. Not one of us has been to church since you were here a year ago." Bishop Tuttle smiled. It is said that he could smile in the face of all kinds of discouragement. He smiled and then changed the subject. Before he left town, however, he had made some changes in the vestry.

Judge Woody is a staunch defender of that vestry. He says that it was a good one, despite appearances, which, he admits, are a little against the members. He says that, while it is true that none of the members of this vestry ever passed the plate at church service, they at least attended to the business affairs of the church and spent for its benefit the money that other people collected. He avers solemnly that two members of the next vestry that was formed bought a Parkes shotgun and a gold watch with the proceeds of the plate collections. As one of these members is now absent from town in the service of the government's forest preserve system and as the other has worn out the gun, it is perhaps best not to mention their names but, the judge says that his vestry has always been given a reputation that it did not deserve. Whether or not the tale of the judge is true---and the Standard has no desire to stand in contempt of court by saying that it is not---it is certain that these two vestrymen bought, one a gun and the other a watch, about the time that the plate collections had amounted to a goodly sum.

These little incidents go to show the kind of game that the bishop found himself up against when he attempted to get the Missoula church started. That his nature is an admirable one and his disposition altogether to be admired is proved by the fact that he has met these men, those of them, at least, who are alive, and has grasped them by the hand and smiled at them a different sort of smile from the one that he used in that vestry meeting. And the vestrymen have stood pat. They have returned his greeting as cordially as if they had always pulled in line with the bishop and have recalled to his mind without blushing the days when they worked so hard to get the young church started. It is to the credit of the bishop's keen judgement he has not asked any one of these vestrymen if they have attended church since he was last here, many years ago. He would have been fully justified in doing so and he would have evened things up in good style.

July 1899

Note:

<u>Bishop Tuttle</u> held the first Protestant church service in Missoula in 1870. He formed Holy Spirit Episcopal Church which is still in existence in Missoula at 130 S. 6th St. E., next to Hellgate High School. The church was originally located where the Missoula Children's Theater is now (though not in the same building).

<u>Vestrymen</u> are members of the church's vestry or leading body.

The First Fruit Trees in Missoula

(JUDGE FRANK H. WOODY, Missoula)

———

You expressed a desire that I should give you some facts concerning the fruit trees that I planted and grow upon the land where my former residence was situated, on the corner of Pine and Higgins avenue. There is not much to tell about them.

I moved onto the place with my family on September, 1873, and in the spring of 1874 I purchased four cherry trees and a half a dozen apple trees and planted them out. They were purchased from a man who came here from Ogden, Utah. They cost me $1.25 each. The four cherry trees that I bought were of a small red variety, the name of which I do not know. I planted them, they grew and came into bearing a few years after, and continued to bear until I sold the place two years since.

Mr. F. L. Worden, the same year, bought from the same man the same kind of cherry trees and planted them in his garden on ground on which the Western Montana National Bank now stands. To the best of my knowledge the cherry trees planted by me, and also by Mr. Worden, were the only cherry trees then planted and growing in the City of Missoula: at the time I purchased the cherry trees from the Ogden man, I purchased half a dozen apple trees, the variety I do not know; but they were of inferior quality, and but few of them lived. A few years after I purchased other fruit trees from the Geneva Nursery, paying $1.25 a-piece for the trees, some were apple trees of the Duchess variety, and some other varieties, the names of which I do not know; also, some plum trees and two Sickls pear tree. These pear trees grew and flourished and bore pears for three or four years. The fruit was small but of a delicious flavor and ripened about the 15th of August. After bearing three or four years, we had a very warm spell during the early part of the month of March of on year, and afterwards, the latter part of March, we had a heavy freeze. The pear trees, when the weather turned warm, put forth leaves, but of a weak, sickly color, and in a short time they died.

I think the cause of the death of the trees was that the warm weather in the early part of March of that year started the sap, and when the cold spell came on the last of March they froze.

I also planted two or three plum trees which did remarkably well for a few years, when finally two of them died. When I sold the place, about two years since, there were three Dutchess apple trees on the place, full bearing, four cherry trees, and two of other apple trees, the names of which I do not know: also two fine large pear trees. After I sold the place the party to whom it was sold neglected to irrigate during the summer and fall, and finally some of them died. It was painful to me to pass by there and see the fruit trees that I had spent so much time and labor in raising drying up. In the spring of 1874 I planted out all of the Cottonwood trees that formed the grove around my residence. Many of them when planted were small, and when cut down some of them were over two feet in diameter. I had one fine Transcendent Crab tree, which was a tall and beautiful tree, but unfortunately I built an addition to my stable, with a board floor, and the drainage from the stable saturated the ground around this tree and before I noticed it the tree began to wither and soon died, cause, evidently, from the replication of the kind of fertilizer that came from the stable.

This is about all I can tell with reference to the orchard inquired about.

Montana Horticultural Society, 1908

Notes:

The Missoula valley was mostly prairie before white settlers arrived. Most (if not all) of the trees you see now in town were brought from other places. The large red fox squirrels you see about town are also transplants that started showing up in the early 1980's.

Judge Woody

Judge Woody and E.S. Paxson (famous western artist)

in front of Old Hellgate Trading Post in 1910

(From Archival Photographs from the University of Montana # 76.0023)

Sarah Countryman Woody as a young woman
Note the cane she used due to injuries from falling
into a campfire as a child.

Society of Montana Pioneers - Group Photo Taken in 1910
Judge Woody is #13 in the front

1 W. F. Bartlett
2 Lou P Smith
3 Granville Stuart — 1857
4 Chas McDermott
5 James McGovern
6 E. W. French
7 John Work
8 John C Innes
9 A. F. Graeter
10 Ed A. Lewis
11 John Neubert
12 Conrad Kohrs
13 Frank H. Woody 1856
14 A. H. Gallup
15 James Mansfield
16 Wb H. Gott
17 Narciss Ledoux
18 Geo W. Morse (bal)

Woody Home on corner of Orange St. and Pine St.
Note St. Francis Xavier Church is across the street.

(From Archival Photographs from the University of Montana # 92.0255)

Photograph of Judge Woody in his mature years

JUDGE WOODY ONCE WAS ONE OF 'EM

Journalism in the West in the early days of Montana was not always the most alluring profession that one might have wished. Editors labored under difficulties and privations of which the present generation has but a faint idea. Mails were at first weekly and, later on, tri-weekly, and in the winter we were often 10 days without an eastern or a California paper from which to steal our editorials, and clip our news items, but when we did get one, and made our clippings from it, the exchange looked as if it had been struck by repeated discharges of a Gatling gun. While we had many disadvantages we were fortunate in some respects. In those early days few of the general readers of our weekly papers ever read the eastern or California papers, and when we were pushed for time or could find no suitable subject for an editorial, we resorted to "royal seizure" and appropriated an able editorial from some of the exchanges which our readers never saw, and which editorials were read by our patrons with very much interest. I remember very well when we received the news of the death of Napoleon III, in 1872. I wanted to write an editorial about him and give a short sketch of his career, but there was not a work of reference in town. Fortunately, the San Francisco Chronicle, which we received, contained an account of his death and also an elaborate editorial on his life and achievements, and from this I constructed an editorial that would have astonished the editor who wrote the one for the Chronicle.

These pilferings were hardly legitimate, but were excusable under the plea of "military necessity." In the early days the editors of many of our weekly papers were not only editors, but "local," and often proprietors, and they were required to furnish not only the copy, but the means to keep the paper running---which was not always easy to do when we shipped our paper by express to Missoula from Helena at 12 ½ cents per pound, cash down, before we could get it out of the express office. Talk about "steamer day!" No one ever hustled on steamer day as we were compelled to on the day when the express arrived with our week's supply of paper. We never failed to get our paper out of the express office, but it sometimes made us sweat blood to do it. I doubt if any other newspaper men in Montana ever had a harder time to meet all requirements than on the editor and proprietors of the Missoulian during the years of 1872 and 1874. In those days there was never a circus in the vicinity. There were few shows of any kind, and complimentary tickets to such entertainments were never seen by the editorial "staff".

In those days, while we did not get any complimentaries, and but little wedding cake and wine, we received our regular supply of threatened lickings, and the kickers of those days were more robust, muscular and dangerous than the kickers of the present time. Most of them wore six-shooters which had a decidedly ugly look. It was not always safe to write what we deemed to be a complimentary personal, and on more than one occasion I raised a storm by printing what I deemed an innocent local. I wrote a harmless item—as I thought—concerning some school marms who were coming to Missoula to spend a portion of their vacation and incidentally mentioned that a bachelor of the town, hearing of that intended visit of these school marms, had caused a new picket fence to be constructed around his bachelor quarters in order to protect himself from invasion. Now, I thought this exceedingly clever, but just here I made a mistake. The bachelor friend was highly indignant and did not speak to me for more than a month and when I received the next number of the New Northwest of Deer Lodge. It contained a letter from one of the aforesaid school marms, in which she walked all over me with spikes in her shoes. This was a good opening, and in our next issue I returned to the fray a little, just vigorously enough to get the lady to go another bout. She came back sharper than ever in the next issue of the New Northwest — and thus it went until Captain Mills shut her off, and that ended the fight.

About this time there was quite a sensation in New York city concerning the "Little Church Around the Corner." At that time of which I write, Dr. T. C. Iliff, now of Salt Lake City, was stationed in Missoula, as a Methodist minister, and was quite a young man. He had in the summer of 1872 erected the church in Missoula now known as the Methodist church and during the winter of 1872-73 he, with some other preachers, were holding a protracted meeting in the church. They had quite a revival. One day, during the time the meeting was in progress, I wrote a short local notice of it, in which I referred to the revival in the little church around the corner, and said something to the effect that Brother Iliff had brought into the fold "Tapioca" and some other tough cases, and that, having succeeded so well with these, there was still hope for "Yeast Powder Bill" and some others in town.

Be it known that there were then in town two rather hard cases, known by these titles. "Tapioca" joined the church and became a bright and shining light--for a short time. Well, Brother Iliff and my other Methodist friends took great umbrage at my little item and appointed a committee, headed by Brother Iliff, to wait on me and demand some kind of a retraction, all of which they did not get. However, the storm soon blew over and Brother Iliff and I have ever since been the warmest kind of friends. Such were a few of the amenities of early journalism in the Wild and Wooly West.

FRANK H. WOODY
September 1899

Notes:

Steamer Day refers to the rush to send and receive correspondence on the steamer ships that sailed between New York and San Francisco. Steamer day in San Francisco occurred on the 1st and 16th of every month.

Captain Mills was the editor of the New Northwest Newspaper in Deerlodge.

The Little Church Around the Corner refers to an episcopal church in New York City called the Church of the Transfiguration. The church earned its nickname from a story repeated from its website:

Legend has it that the unusual nickname comes from 1870, when the stage actor Joseph Jefferson, famous for his portrayal of Rip Van Winkle, sought to bury his friend and fellow actor, George Holland. Approaching the priest of a neighboring church, Jefferson was turned away. During the 19th century, acting as a profession was somewhat frowned upon, hence the priest's refusal to bury Holland. The disapproving priest suggested that, "there is a little church around the corner where it might be done." According to the legend of the church, Jefferson is thought to have replied, "Then I say to you sir, God bless the little church around the corner.".

WHEN JUDGE WOODY WAS EDITOR

TIME OF HIS RESIGNATION CALLED TO MIND BY STORY IN MADISONIAN

Missoula people will remember Frank Conway, who was for some time a member of the editorial staff of the Missoulian and who for the past few years has been with the Anaconda Standard at its Butte office. Recently Mr. Conway went to Virginia City to assume editorial charge of the Madisonian, the pioneer paper of Montana.

A few days ago the following communication was received from Mr. Conway, which will be of interest here:

"I am acting as editor for the Madisonian, also enjoying my vacation, the first one in two years, by working a little harder than usual. In going over the files of the first volume of the Madisonian of 37 years ago, I find the following story of interest to Missoulians, which I am sending you."

From Madisonian

The story in the Madisonian appeared under the caption, "Newspaper Changes Hands," and is as follows;

"Frank Woody, editor of the Missoulian, died an editorial death last week. He printed his own obituary and said he died for private purposes and commercial reasons. He leaves the Missoulian to the supervision and control of his former partner, towit:

"Warren R. Turk, ESQ., will assume full control of the Missoulian, both as editor and publisher, and, being a vigorous writer and a practical printer, the patrons of the paper may rest assured that they will continue to receive a paper well worthy of their support."

"After this, he says adieu to the rest of us paste-pot and scissors lights in the following touching tribute, which is accepted:

"'To our brethren of the paste pot and pencil of the territorial press we tender our sincere thanks for the many kindnesses and courtesies received at their hands.'

"We hope our friend Turk may never be a 'Sick Turk,' and 'laboring like a Turk' will continue to make the Missoulian a lively and interesting sheet."

This little story was printed on Saturday, March 14, 1874. When Tom Deyarmon was the proprietor of the Madisonian and John R. Wilson was the local and associate editor.

December 1910

LIKE A DREAM

––––––––

"It seems like a dream---like a dream." Over and over, Dr. Thomas Corwin Iliff, Missoula's first preacher, repeated this yesterday, as he viewed the city in which his first parish work was done, 40 years ago. "I am lost," he said to the Man About Town, as he shook hands in the hearty way which is his characteristic. "Of course, I have seen Missoula once or twice since we lived here, but the memory which I have had of the place has always been the little town which I knew in 1871 and the transformation has been wonderful. Yes, the old church corner is there yet, but it doesn't seem like the same place. When I selected it---they left it to me – it seemed a long way out. Some of our people thought it was too far out. But now it is right in town. It belonged to Walter Johnson; he was a young man in the government service and was in Helena when I found him. He didn't want to sell the lot; he said he had intended it for a homestake. But I told him the church had to have it and he let it go, after a while. But how the town has changed! What a beautiful city it has grown to be! It seems indeed like a dream."

THE OLD PEOPLE

"But there are some of the same old people here," continued Dr. Iliff. "I have met a few of them already and they make it seem a little like home. I met Willie

Cave just now on the street. I knew him right away. I remember when I married his father and mother---Alf Cave was a fine man. And that wedding was a long time ago. I have always remembered the Missoulian. Frank Woody was its editor in those days and he and his family were our warmest friends. They were very kind to us. I remember once when two notorious characters, 'Tapioca' and 'Yeast Powder Bill,' had been in trouble--- Woody suggested in his paper that they should be induced to join our church---he called it 'The Little Church on the Corner.' Well, I saw his joke and was smiling over it when some of the good sisters came to see me about it. They didn't see any joke about it and I couldn't persuade them that it was not wise to get into a controversy with the editor. It was a serious matter to them. So I consented and we went around to see Frank Woody. We stated our grievance and he agreed to apologize. But you should have seen that apology. It seemed to satisfy the sisters, but it always appeared to me that the apology was a good deal worse than the first statement. I never was very much for fighting with editors, anyway."

October 1911

THE HISTORY OF THE RESERVATION IS TEEMING WITH INTEREST

The Flathead Indian reservation was established with its present boundaries at a treaty held on July 16, 1855, in a large pine grove about eight miles below Missoula, in what is now called Grass valley. The treaty was made by Isaac I. Stevens, governor and ex-officio superintendent of Indian affairs of the territory of Washington, and the chiefs and head men of the Flathead, Kootenay and upper Pend d'Oreille Indians. The treaty was not ratified by the senate of the United States until March 8, 1859 and was generally known as the Stevens treaty.

The pine grove in which the treaty was consummated was for a number of years known as Council Grove. All or nearly all of the persons who were present at that treaty have since passed to the great beyond. About three years ago the writer had occasion to look up some evidence in regard to certain facts of this treaty, and, in order to determine these facts, commenced making inquiries for the persons whose names are attached to the document, as witnesses or interpreters. The only white persons he could find who were present at the treaty were Hazzard Stevens, a son of Governor Stevens, a boy of 16 at the time the treaty was signed, and now a practicing lawyer in the city of Boston, and a gentleman named W. H. Tappan who is now a very old man and resided in the state of

Massachusetts. He also found three Indians who were present and participated in the treaty---Francois Eneas, Louis Vanderburg and Charlois, the present chief of the Flatheads.

Their depositions were taken to be used in a case then pending in the United States court, and each one of them testified that he was present at the treaty held, heard all that was said and remembered everything distinctly, and Francois Eneas testified that he was assistant interpreter at the council. These Indians are still living on the Flathead reservation, although Francois is now blind.

At the time of the treaty the Flathead tribe, which was then living in the Bitter Root valley, was not disposed to move to the present reservation, as the Bitter Root had always been their home. To satisfy Victor, chief of the Flatheads, an additional article was inserted in the treaty and numbered article 11. Concerning the correct interpretation of this treaty there has been a great deal of litigation. The article follows:

"It is moreover provided that the Bitter Root valley, above the Loo Lo fork shall be carefully surveyed and examined and if it shall prove, in the judgement of the president, to be better adapted to the wants of the Flathead tribe than the general reservation provided for in the treaty, then such portions of it as may be necessary shall be set apart as a separate reservation for said tribe. No portion of the Bitter Root valley above the Loo Lo fork shall be open to settlement until such examination is had and the decision of the president is made known."

In 1871 the executive of the nation issued an order finding that the Bitter Root valley was not better adapted to the needs of the Flatheads than the general reservation, and that it was "deemed unnecessary to set apart any portion of said Bitter Root valley as a separate reservation for the Indians referred to in said treaty."

Prior to June 16, 1855, no treaty had ever been made with the Flatheads, Kootenay and Pend d'Oreille Indians, but in 1854 Governor Stevens, the first executive of the territory of Washington, appointed Thomas Adams special agent for the Flatheads. In 1855 the government appointed the first regular agent for the three tribes in the person of Dr. Landsdale of Oregon. Since the time of the treaty the three Indian tribes have been known as the Confederated Tribe of the Flathead Nation of Indians.

In the latter part of the year 1855 Dr. Lansdale came up from Oregon and established his agency on the present Flathead reservation at or near the mouth of the Jocko river and in the immediate vicinity of the present Northern Pacific station called Dixon. In the spring of 1856 Dr. Landsdale went to Salt Lake City on business connected with the agency, returning in the early summer.

In the fall of 1855 a young man named Henry G. Miller from New York state came to Utah and spent the winter of that year at a Mormon settlement, the present city of Ogden. While there he fell in love with a young Mormon girl and, he being a Gentile, the Mormons would not consent to the marriage. In the spring of 1856 Miller and the young lady escaped on horseback from the Mormon settlement and made their way to Fort Hall, a trading post owned by the Hudson Bay company. This fort was in what is now the state of Idaho and was in charge of Captain Richard Grant, who was the father of Mrs. Julia P. Higgins, now living near the city of Missoula.

The young couple were received at the fort and there someone, by what authority the writer does not know, performed a marriage ceremony for them. There they remained until the arrival of Dr. Landsdale, who was on his return to the Flathead reservation from Salt Lake. Dr. Landsdale engaged Miller and his young wife to go with him to the reservation and take charge of it during his absence in Oregon. They made the journey from Fort Hall to the mouth of the Jocko on horseback. The lady's name after the marriage was Mrs. Minnie Miller. She was the second white woman ever within the limits of what is now the state of Montana and positively the first that ever took up residence. The white women that preceded her simply passed through the country from Winnipeg, crossing the state somewhere through Tobacco Plains to Colville. Miller and his wife remained at this Jocko agency---as it was then called---until the fall of 1857, when they removed to Walla Walla. At that time the agency consisted of only a few log cabins. Mrs. Miller lived there from her arrival in 1856 until she departed in the fall of 1857 without ever seeing another white woman.

Dr. Landsdale went to Portland, Oregon, later in the fall of 1857, and, as to whether or not he ever returned to the agency, the writer has no knowledge. In 1860 Major John Owen was appointed Indian agent to succeed Dr. Landsdale. After Major Owen was appointed he kept his office for the transaction of the business of the agency at his trading post, Fort Owen, in the Bitter Root valley, near the present town of Stevensville. During the summer of 1860 he established a new agency on the present reservation and employed a number of men in constructing the agency's buildings on the creek about one mile below the site of the present agency.

During that summer he commenced the construction of a dam and built a sawmill on the Jocko river, about two or three miles above the present agency. The sawmill was constructed by a millwright named Daniel Calkins. It was a good, substantial affair and in it was placed the first saw within the limits of Montana. A large force of men was employed on the reservation at that time, Milton W. Tipton being in charge as head foreman, and a number of hands were employed at the mill to cut lumber. After several years of use this mill was destroyed by fire and never rebuilt. Major Owen after serving as Indian agent for two or three years, either was removed or resigned, and the writer is under the impression that he was removed for political reasons, he being a democrat and the administration of the United States at that time republican.

Charles Hutchins was appointed agent February 20, 1864, to succeed Major Owen and held the position until some time in 1865. He was succeeded by A. H. Chapman who was appointed in September, 1865, and held the place until some time in 1866, when he was suspended. Major W. J. McCormick was appointed special agent and held the position until November, 1866, when he was relieved by the appointment of John W. Wells, who held office until July 25, 1868, when he was succeeded by Major M. M. McCauley of Missoula, who held the position until the spring of 1869, at which time the reservation was placed under the jurisdiction of the war department. Major A. S. Galbreath was detailed to take charge of the reservation on June 11, 1869, and was relieved in 1870 by Lieutenant G. E. Ford, U. S A., who was succeeded on September 9, 1870, by Charles S. Jones. In 1872 Jones was suspended and on November 15, 1872, Daniel Shanahan was appointed agent, holding the position until some time in 1874, when he resigned, his being the only resignation of any head of this agency on record. On May 2, 1874, Major Peter Whaley, now a resident of Missoula, was appointed agent to fill the vacancy caused by the resignation of Agent Shanahan, and filled the office until some time in 1875, when he was succeeded by Major Charles S. Medary, who was appointed on April 30, 1875. Major Medary held the position until he was succeeded by Major Peter Ronan, whose term of office---16 years--- is the longest of any agent in charge of the reservation. And he gave better satisfaction to the Indians and the government than any other agent who occupied the same position. He was succeeded by Major Joseph Carter, who held the place until he was relieved by the appointment of Major W. H. Smead, now of Missoula, who held the place four or five years, until he was relieved by the appointment of Major Samuel Bellew of Missoula. Major Bellew held the position until the summer of 1908, when he was succeeded by Major Fred C. Morgan, the present agent.

I believe the foregoing is a correct and complete roster of all the persons who have ever held the position of agent for the Confederated Tribes of the Flathead, Kootenay and Upper Pend D'Oreille Indians, known as the Flathead Nation.

It is a well known fact and one not to the credit of the United States that the government has ever since the making of the Stevens treaty in July, 1855, willfully failed and neglected to carry out the terms of the treaties made with the three tribes. The first annuities were shipped up the Missouri river to Fort Benton in the summer of 1860 and were transported by wagons to Fort Owen in the Bitter Root valley in the fall of the same year. These supplies consisted, among other things, of several hundred boxes of army hard tack and several hundred sacks of rice, more of which were sold to the white settlers than were ever delivered to the Indians.

In 1872 J. A. Garfield as a special agent, made a treaty with the Flathead tribe of these Indians and the terms of the agreement were never carried out. Later on, General Carrington, an officer of the United States army, was delegated with authority to make another treaty with the Flathead tribe, looking to their removal from the Bitter Root valley to the present reservation, and the terms and provisions of this treaty were never fulfilled by the government.

If any tribe of Indians has ever had reason to complain of the noncompliance of treaty stipulations and bad faith on the part of the government, the Flathead tribe certainly has.

FRANK H. WOODY
May 1909

Note:

The article above this in the newspaper was titled:

"President Taft's Official Word Opens the Reservation to Homesteading May 22, 1909."

JUDGE WOODY TALKS OF UNCLE JOE

The Missoula Pioneer Met the Speaker of the House in Indiana in the Fifties

Judge Frank H. Woody and other members of the Hard Rock Pioneer club met up on the steps of the Western Montana Bank building yesterday and indulged in reminiscences.

"Way back in the 50's," said Judge Woody, "I went to school at New Garden, S. C. On leaving there I taught in the backwoods of Wayne county for $20 a month. That was my first experience on my own hook. I had never had to shift for myself. Board and washing cost me $4.50. That was the cheapest fare I ever got. I completed my three months and drove down to Goldsboro for my money. After passing a hard examination, I was paid off in $10 bills."

"I shall never forget that day; that was my first cash. On the way back home I took it out of my pocket and looked at it a dozen different times."

"The next year I moved into Wilson county, on Toss Not swamp, and taught for $25. There my board, washing, a horse to ride on Sunday, or any other time when he was not busy, and a negro to wait on me cost me $5 a month. Those were good days for me. Sometimes I think I was a fool for quitting that job, but if I had remained there I might have been shot to pieces at Malvern Hill or somewhere else."

"What made you come west?"

Came West

"I had the western fever, and many of my people had gone to Indiana to live. I wanted to go to California. Therefore, I started out. I went to Portsmouth, Va. Took a boat to Baltimore, and then boarded a train for Cincinnati. There were but few railroads in those days. I attended a Quaker school in the Hoosier state for a while and then went to Annapolis, that state, to teach.

"It was there that I met Joe Cannon, speaker of the House of Representatives. He was clerking in one of the four corner stores of the village. I used to go and sit around his stove with other loafers. Joe was a very studious sort of chap. I remember that he would read at nights and on Sundays, when we would permit it. That was in 1853."

"I made another move, that time landing in Utah, where I had two bitter years. At the end of that time a party of us started for California, and had an insurrection on the train. Nine or ten of us struck. That was about the first strike in this country. I have always believed that I was one of the first strikers, as well as one of the first tramps, that ever came west. Finally, I wound up here, and here I am today."

In Utah

"Well, sir, on quitting Annapolis I lost track of everybody there. I did not hear from anybody in that community. But, many years after I arrived in Missoula a man by the name of Lamb came out from Chicago, to collect some claims for banks, and when he brought his troubles to me, I asked him where he hailed from originally. I had my suspicions from the twang that rolled from his silver lips."

"'North Carolina – Randolph county,' was his answer.

"That fellow had been to Indiana and knew all of the people of Annapolis. I asked him about Joe Cannon.

"'Why,' he said, 'he is in congress.'

"I knew that there was a congressman by the name of Cannon but I had not the remotest idea that it was my old friend Joe."

"At that time, Martin McGinnis and Joe Toole were the Montana delegates in congress, and I told them to ascertain for me if the Cannon there was the boy that used to clerk, in Sam Enzy's store, and see if he recalled me. That was the beginning of a sort of oral communication between us. Later, we got to writing to one another. I had a long letter from Joe one Christmas."

Saw Uncle Joe

"Several years later, he and one of his daughters passed through here on their way to the coast. At Helena he wired me to meet him at the station. I took one of my daughters and went down. When the train stopped, I searched through all of the Pullman cars for a man that I thought looked like Joe Cannon, but my efforts were in vain. The conductor said that he did not have any congressmen on board. Well, when I was ready to give up, I saw a dapper–looking fellow wearing a pair of steel-rimmed glasses and a gray suit, and was about to speak to him when he inquired: 'Are you Judge Woody?'

"That was Joe, but I could not recognize a single feature. The more he talked the more I knew that he was the Joe Cannon of '53, with many years added to his life. We had so much to talk about that I did not know where to start. Naturally, we drifted back to Annapolis, and brought up old times and old people.

"'How in the h—l did you get away out here?' he asked me. I told him about my rambles.

"Then I asked, 'Joe, how in the h—l did you end up in Congress?'

Trials

"He told me a most interesting story. Soon after I left Indiana, he went to Terra Haute and studied law with a firm there. Later, he spent six months in a law school in Cincinnati, but had to give up the course because of a lack of funds. From there he drifted back to Terra Haute, penniless and unsettled. He wanted to go to Chicago, but didn't have the railroad fare. Becoming desperate, he climbed into a west-bound train, and waited for developments. The conductor came around to take up his ticket.

"'I have none,'said the young fellow.

"'Give me the money,'demanded the conductor.

"'I have no money,' was the reply.

"'Where then, would you go with no money or ticket?' inquired the trainman.

"Joe told him his purpose. By that time the train was on the way. The conductor looked his passenger over and observed 'You've got no business over at Chicago. I will drop you off up here and let you go to work on a farm, where you can make $15 a month and stay out of mischief.'

Had to Farm

"He was as good as his word. Joe was let down in a prosperous farming community and there he went to work. From what he told me, it was about 10 years before he got down to business. Every chance he got he would draw up a legal paper. Step by step he climbed the ladder. He said that when once on the go he kept moving.

"'Yes old fellow,' he said, 'when I learned how it was easy.'

"That's the kind of stuff the early pioneers had. It was odd that we two Tar Heels, born in the same settlement, should have drifted together in that way. His parents carried him to Indiana when he was two years old. I came of my own accord before I was of age. I am several years older than Joe."

July 1910

Notes:

Joseph Gurney Cannon ("Uncle Joe") was the Speaker of the U.S. House of Representatives from 1903-1911. He was a Republican representing the state of Illinois.

The Battle of Malvern Hill was a Civil War battle that occurred on July 1, 1862. The confederacy took heavy casualties. Judge Woody escaped having to serve in the Confederate Army by moving west.

CELESTIAL RETURNS FOR FRIENDLY VISIT

A.H. Hay, formerly a resident of Missoula and a man who is prominently known in the Chinese community, is spending a few days visiting with friends before leaving for Seattle, where he will purchase goods of oriental design and make for a store in which he is interested in Kalispell. It is 17 years since Mr. Hay left Missoula to take up a residence in Flathead county, and since that time his visits have not been many.

He came to Missoula first 30 years ago, being then a lad of eight years of age, and was accompanied by his uncle, Hun Buck Jim, who is now a merchant in Deer Lodge, carrying a large line of Chinese and Japanese made goods. The pair came direct to Missoula from China and they remained in this city together, until the uncle finally decided to make a move. Mr. Hay always lived with the family of Judge Frank H. Woody, and it is in the Woody home that the prosperous Chinese merchant is now visiting.

November 1910

Notes:

"Celestial Visitor" is a reference to an old name for China, Celestial Kingdom. In the 19th century, Chinese visitors to the United States were often referred to as "Celestials".

Ah Hay or the Americanized A.H. Hay and his uncle emigrated to the United States in 1880 and Ah Hay moved in with the Woody family after his uncle relocated to Butte, MT. He stayed with the Woodys for several years and helped out around the house while attending public school. His tenure with the Woodys enabled him to learn to write and speak English perfectly. He eventually moved out on his own and opened a vegetable farming business. Later on, he moved to Kalispell and opened a Chinese store and restaurant. He ended up working for the Great Northern Railway, operating restaurants, and hotels. He was a shrewd businessman and ended up quite well off. He returned to China in 1939 at the age of 70 and left his two sons to oversee his interests in the United States.

MISSOULA THEN & NOW

1865 – 1911

Down the river four miles there is Hell Gate. There is a low building there, made of hewn cottonwood logs mud-chinked, serviceable and warm yet despite the weather of half a century and more, and in daily use, as granary and storehouse. This building is the store Worden & Co., Frank L. Worden and C.P. Higgins. It was the first mercantile establishment anywhere near Missoula and it was established in 1860. In it was sold everything literally, groceries, clothes, hardware and anything else the pioneers of western Montana could ask for. In August, 1860, the store was opened. Judge Frank H. Woody was clerk there from 1860 to the spring of 1862. Then he quit and the two proprietors worked alone until April in 1864. Then, for a year, Judge Woody, who, of course, hadn't even dreamed of becoming Judge Woody then, came back to the store. In 1865 James P. Reinhard---"Jimmy" Reinhard---came out from Missouri and the store was moved to Missoula, which wasn't Missoula at all then but Missoula Mills. The store was moved, says Judge Woody, about the last of November or the first of December.

"Reinhard worked there quite a while," says Judge Woody, "and in 1868 he went into business for himself. Then, Worden & Co. had a whole generation of clerks. This store, once it had been moved to Missoula

Mills, was on West Front street---where doors below what is now the Florence hotel block."

The store continued, of course, to handle a general stock and to do a trading business with the ranchers and other inhabitants of the country. All of its goods were shipped from St. Louis up the Missouri river or were packed in from Walla Walla. In 1864, again according to Judge Woody, the annual consignment for the Missoula Mills store started up the river but grounded at Nebraska City whence it was hauled in by bull teams. That year there must have been close figuring and a lack of cove oysters, which constituted the chief delicacy and extravagance of the times. Cove oysters sold for $1.50 a can and were frequently stakes in games of "Seven up" played in the old store.

Judge Woody doesn't think that the old timers drank any more than do the men of today, but he says, they did drink. When they did, they paid $9.00 a gallon for their whiskey and a popular fad was to encourage thirst by eating cove oysters. This, it must be said, made carousels in the olden days rather expensive.

Then, there are other prices that make the present day cost of living seem very modest. The first people of Missoula Mills and western Montana paid $1 for a linen handkerchief without a murmur and spent $2.50 with equal cheerfulness when they wanted one of silk. A box of matches cost 25 cents and a plug of tobacco 75 cents. A white shirt was worth $5.00 and trousers ran all the way from $11 to $16. Overalls cost $3.50 a pair, "and they were not as good overalls as we get today, I reckon," says Judge Woody.

An old day-book of the Missoula Mills store kept by "Jimmy" Reinhard and now the property of W.C. Murphy, gives the prices quoted above along with a lot more just as interesting. Also, it gives a picture of life in the '60s in Missoula Mills and lets us know how the first settlers lived. The ranchers "ran a bill" at the store until after harvest, they came in and settled up, getting $4 a bushel for their wheat and receiving proportionate prices for other produce. The old journal tells, also, something of, the social life. A day or so ago Judge Woody was looking through the book. He saw that one day's sales included several white shirts---price $5---and numerous pairs of trousers----worse than that a lot---and that there had been a run on neckties and handkerchiefs. "Ah," said he, "there was a dance that night."

Then came Christmas days, 1866. "Jimmy" Reinhard charged a lot of oysters to himself, along with a box of cigars and sundry other luxuries and a lot of the male inhabitants---and the population was about all male---bought shirts and hats in great numbers. L. McLarin came in and bought two window shades. Then, evidently, he changed his mind, for the entry is scratched and underneath there is; "One gallon whiskey, $9."

The real Christmas celebration, if a selfish one, was put on by A. Babb of whom Judge Woody can remember nothing. He bought an overcoat for $42, a dress coat for $35, a vest for $8, two handkerchiefs for $3, one hat for $9, one necktie for 75 cents, a pair of drawers for $3, two linen shirts for $10, one pair of boots for $12, one bottle of sweet oil for $2, one bottle of perfume for $2, three plugs of tobacco for $2.25, one pair of trousers for $14, another hat, "for dad," for $7 and a white shirt for $4.50. His bill amounted to $156.60. He was the banner customer for the day. On the day after Christmas L. McLarin paid $7.50 for a looking glass probably to determine whether or not he looked as bad as he felt. Clerk Reinhard had noted in pencil on the margin of the book that the snow was eight inches deep on that Christmas day.

That was a tough winter too, for the journal says, again in marginal penciling, that on March 21 the snow was two feet deep all over the valley, with several inches in town, while the river was frozen to the depth of half a foot. Two days later the thermometer registered 14 degrees below zero. The cold spell didn't last long however, for a note made on the 25th reads, "Bright and pleasant."

There is another source of information in the old book, however. It gives what is practically a census of the town and the country surrounding. The store was really a clearing house and through it the people lived to a great degree. From the rich storehouse that is his memory Judge Woody has given the following facts concerning the old-timers who traded at the old store:

Abram Haney came from the east, having made the trip around the Horn. He was an especial friend of Mr. Worden, the two being great chums. Haney was a carpenter and remained here two or three years before he returned east.

"Billy" Stevens, Judge Woody says, ran a hotel at what is now the intersection of Pattee and Front street. He was improvident and was always in debt. He went from Missoula to Idaho, where he died.

David Pattee came here in a very early day. He traded at Fort Owen in 1857 and in Missoula Mills. When Worden & Co. started their store, in 1860, they bought from him the cottonwood logs of which the store was built. He had a farm up Pattee canyon, named for him, as is a city street. He spent the evening of his life in Los Angeles.

Harding brothers have many an entry against them in the old book. The brothers, Anning and Dwight, came from Pennsylvania. They did various things running a butcher shop for a time. Both died here.

Pat Bray, says the judge, was an Irishman from Minnesota, a miner in Deer Lodge county. Pat came to Missoula for his supplies.

Pierre M. Lafountaine was known as "Johnny Crapeau." He came to Missoula---what is now Missoula---in 1856 from Canada and is now living on the east side of the Bitter Root river in this county.

R. M. Biggs was a carpenter, but worked at anything he could get to do. He took up a ranch on Grant creek, afterward the property of John Rankin and part of the Rankin estate, and then drifted away.

C.C. Edmundson was a pioneer of the '60s. He took up the ranch now known as the "Cold Springs ranch," got a patent to it and then went to Arkansas.

Weller and Dyer, appearing on the book as a firm, had the first blacksmith's shop here. Both left the county for eastern Montana.

E. L. Bonner and D. J. Welch were, really, the founders of the present Missoula Mercantile company. They ran a store here and after Welch withdrew from the partnership, Bonner took in <u>A.B. Hammond and R. A. Eddy</u>. Welch went to Butte, where he was elected county treasurer. He died there.

<u>L. Kirshner</u> was known as "Dad" by the system of nicknames that spared but few of the men of the early days. He was a carpenter. He returned to Columbus, Ohio, his home.

<u>Henry Buckhouse</u> came to Hell Gate in 1864. He was a smith. He had a ranch near the present city. There his widow and children reside now.

<u>Jack Comstock</u> was a laborer and prospector. The store records show that he was a most consistent drinker. He left here for Fort Benton and disappeared, as far as Missoula Mills was concerned.

<u>J. B. Lavallee</u> was an old-country Frenchman. He was a smith and had a ranch on Lavallee creek above De Smet. When he sold this ranch he moved to Frenchtown, where he died.

<u>George P. White</u> lived on a ranch five miles below town. He was a rancher and afterward ran a store at Hell Gate. He was the father of <u>"Chick" White</u>.

<u>John Gregory</u> came from Walla Walla and opened a blacksmith shop, although he was not a smith himself. The name of his partner has been lost. A child of Gregory was drowned in the flume that supplied water to old mill from the Rattlesnake. He returned to Walla Walla.

The nickname of John McKay was "Brady". He was a carpenter.

Milo Russell was a shoemaker. He was a married man and lived in a cabin on West Front street.

E. L. Newell was a millwright, the principal artisan in the construction of the mill that gave Missoula part of its first name.

M. W. Tipton lived on a ranch two mile the other side of Frenchtown. From there he went to Pueblo, Colo., where he contracted smallpox and died.

Moses Reeves worked about town and had a grist mill above Frenchtown.

Louis Brown, "No. 1" was an old Canadian hunter and trapper of the Kit Carson type. At Colville, Wash., he had married an Indian woman and in '58 he came to Frenchtown. Later he moved to the reservation. Going home one night from Ravalli, after the Northern Pacific came through, he was run over and killed.

George M. Windes, whose name appears many times in the old book, was one of the millwrights in the force that built the mill here.

Then, there is W. B. Higgins, "William Bolivar Shakespeare," was his nickname says Judge Woody. He was a Yankee and no relation to the Higgins family still represented here. He married a sister of F. L. Worden. From here he went to Winnipeg, then settled on the Yellowstone, finally going to California. There he died.

The names of <u>Fred Loveland</u> and <u>Henry P. Larrabee</u> appear in the old book as a firm. They were ranchers up Pattee canyon. Larrabee was the first regularly elected sheriff after the county was organized. He left Missoula for Missouri or Arkansas before he died, says Judge Woody. Loveland spent the evening of his life in Illinois.

<u>Anderson</u> and <u>Thayer</u> were lawyers of Lewiston, Idaho, who prospected in western Montana and spent a winter here. Anderson died at Globe, Arizona, and Thayer finished his career at Portland.

<u>Louis Clairmont</u> was an American Fur company man, who worked about Fort Owen. He married a halfbreed and took up a ranch on Burnt Fork. Then he moved to the reservation and died there.

<u>Walter W. Johnson</u> was a civil engineer and surveyed the first townships in the county. He went back to Washington and later on, acquired an interest in a mine in Virginia. He fell down a shaft and was killed.

The name of <u>Father Ravalli</u> is in the book many times. The famous priest was in the midst of his active career at that time.

The T. F. Meagher of the day book was <u>General Thomas Francis Meagher</u>, afterward acting governor of the territory. He stepped overboard from a steamer at Fort Benton and his body was never found.

G. W. Dobbins came to the Bitter Root in '62. He conducted a smithy and a saloon for a long time and is now living on the edge of Stevensville. He was known as "Red."

Much has been written of Major John Owen, Indian agent in charge of Fort Owen at Stevensville and a member of the legislature when it met at Virginia City. He came from Philadelphia and died at Camden, N. J., of softening of the brain.

H. W. Miller was the hero of one of the first romances of the Montana frontier. In 1855 he arrived in Utah from New York state, spending that winter in the Mormon settlement, where Ogden now stands. There he fell in love with a young Mormon girl, but, as he was a Gentile, her relatives would not consent to a marriage. In the following spring Miller and the young lady took horses and escaped from the settlement, making their way to Fort Hall, a trading post of the Hudson Bay company.

William Raup, a carpenter, took up 160 acres just above the bridge. The university stands upon part of this land now and the remainder lies in Montana addition. "I bought this from Roup for $1,600 for Captain Higgins," says Judge Woody. Raup went to California.

About R. R. Smith, bartender and musician, there is little to be said.

R. A. Pelkey was a printer from St. Louis, a Frenchman. He learned his trade in the office of the old Missouri Republican. He had been in California in the early days and had worked his way up north, also. He took a Colville Indian woman as his wife and came here in 1860. She ran away and left him with two children. One of them, R. A. Pelkey, Jr., was at one time a newspaper man in Butte. Pelkey had the first hotel here.

A. H Ross was brought out from St. Louis by Mr. Worden to work as a clerk. He was well educated, a man of fine tastes, "and a good clerk," adds Judge Woody. Ross never talked about his family, but there was an understanding that he was the illegitimate son of a British officer, who had educated him. He was of an adventurous turn and in 1872, when the preliminary survey of the Northern Pacific was being made he and several others started down the river in a boat. They encountered rapids on the other side of Frenchtown and the boat was swamped. Ross was drowned. "He had, evidently, had a presentment of his fate," says the judge, "for it was found that he had made a will before he started, leaving all he had to Worden and Higgins."

C. C. O'Keefe was "Baron" O'Keefe. He came with the maker of the Mullan military road and settled on a ranch above the Marent trestle.

Cy McWhirk was a gardener. McWhirk addition was his property.

Matt Adams ranched up the Bitter Root about 20 miles, near where the McClains live. He served as county assessor. He moved from here to Fort Benton and married a squaw.

John H. Harkins was a farm hand of the early days. He went from here to Riverside county, California.

T. W. Harris was an early-day clerk at Fort Owen. He died on his ranch on Three Mile creek.

Bowen and Minesinger---the latter's initials being J. M.---were partners on a ranch. Minesinger took up what is now known as the Lehsou ranch. Also, he platted the first townsite here. He married a Snake Indian woman and his son is now working for the Northern Pacific out of Missoula.

Toft is the name of a German draughtsman and musician. Fifty years have lost his first name. Besides, he was here but one winter.

C. H. Hayden was an Englishman who cooked in the hotel and later opened a livery and feed stable. From here he traveled to the Puget Sound country and went broke. "A cousin of one of the Hardings afterwards saw him on his way to the poor farm," says the judge.

Gus Tebeau was a farm hand who went to Walla Walla from here.

J. S. Caldwell came into the country in 1860 with General Mullan. He settled in Grass valley, on land now owned by Gaspard Deschamps.

Ed Corran was a Canadian, who worked at Fort Benton and then at Fort Owen. With his Flathead wife, he settled on Burnt Fork, afterward moving to the reservation, where he died.

A.H. Chapman ran a livery stable. He was married here and moved to Stevensville, where he acquired a ranch and spent the remainder of his life.

R. Marshall had a ranch between here and Bonner. From here he went to St. Anne, Los Angeles county.

H. Larivie had a hotel at Frenchtown and a ranch near there. He was killed by a falling log while cutting timber on Nine-Mile creek.

E. A. P. Hillman, a French Canadian was a laborer. He died here.

Morgan Spencer was a rancher near Frenchtown. With his father-in-law, Milton W. Tipton, he went to Pueblo and died there.

Ned Williamson made clothes out of buckskin for the old-timers. He died on the Crow reservation.

A.G. England came into this country in 1864 with a packtrain and took up a ranch. He was from Illinois, Judge Woody thinks. He was the father of O. G. England.

Charles McCarty, an old stage driver, took up what is called the Tyler ranch, where he died.

Jack Upton was a prospector.

Moses Duncan was one-fourth negro. He died on his ranch, in what is now the Orchard Homes district.

W. H. Parent lived on a ranch on Grant creek.

Charles Luton, after occupying a ranch about where M. Flynn's place is now, went back east.

Cornelius Coakley owned a ranch near where Charles Winter now lives. He sold this property and moved away.

G. Gallagher was a carpenter without much of a local record.

Pat Shea was an Irish laborer.

Antoine Martineau was a Frenchman from St. Louis. He had a ranch near De Smet and moved to Fort Benton.

E. A. (Sandy) Baugh was a trader, but where he went is as little known as what happened to him.

Gaspard Deschamps is still in business in Missoula, one of the wealthiest men in western Montana.

John Switzer had a half interest in a store at Frenchtown, the first one there.

Oliver & Co. were two Mormons, who ran a stage line between Missoula and Deer Lodge.

Anthony Chaffin was a rancher up the Bitter Root, just above Corvallis. He moved into Yellowstone county.

H. Fox was a packer. He moved onto the Crow reservation and married into the tribe.

F. Bisson was a rancher, living on the north side of the Missoula river between the city and the juncture of the Bitter Root river.

John Fisher was an old miner and prospector from California. He died at Kalispell.

James Woods, a packer, came from Walla Walla and went to Hailey, Idaho.

Champion Kinney was a farmer and freighter. He left his wife here, divorced her and married again at Fort McLeod.

Asbury Plumber ran a livery stable and finally moved onto a ranch near Florence.

John Grant, Captain Grant's son, lived at Deer Lodge. He moved to British Columbia and died there.

John Sullivan lived in a cabin at the end of West Front street. His wife died here and he moved to Wyoming.

L. McLarin was a Scotchman from Canada, a Hudson Bay Man. He married the daughter of Captain Grant, a sister of Mrs. Captain Higgins, and moved back to Minnesota.

W. Bills came here from Colville with an Indian wife. He lived down the valley, on what is now one of the Deschamps ranches. He began to go blind and went to Cincinnati to have his eyes treated. He died there. He was the father of Mrs. J. R. Latimer.

J. R. Latimer was a farmer until several years ago, when he sold his ranch. Mr. Latimer is now a resident of Missoula and a prominent citizen.

"Hank" Cone was a rancher on the Skalkaho. He moved to the Raft river country in southern Idaho.

John Hall was a laborer and freighter. He ran away owing the store between $600 and $700.

William Broderick had a ranch below Frenchtown. He died near Helena.

B. W. Sherman was a rancher and freighter who lived up the Bitter Root, near Corvallis. He moved into Meagher County and grew rich in the cattle business. There he was elected county commissioner.

John Chatfield was a consumptive who came here to die, but couldn't. He ran a saloon at Stevensville and died of old age.

W. H. Jacoby ran the mill. He died here.

Luther Richards lived on a ranch below Frenchtown.

Peter Ranton was a laborer and then a teamster. He was hauling logs on the flat below were the Clark dam now is at Bonner and was crushed to death by a log.

J. B. Spooner was a Frenchman. He owned a ranch up the Bitter Root, where he still lives.

Perry Eldridge was a laborer.

T. M. Pomeroy was justice of the peace, then probate judge and then clerk of the court. He was a masonic grand master and went to Butte to assist in the laying of the corner stone for the Masonic temple there. Coming back something happened to his train and he was forced, with the other passengers, to walk several miles into Deer Lodge. He contracted pneumonia and died there. He owned the property that is now the Union block.

James Donovan, "Little Guy," carried the mail between here and Ponderay lake when W. A. Clark and Warren Whitcher had the contract.

R. A. Eddy was a partner of E. L. Bonner. He is now living in Paris.

Rev. Father Grassi was a priest at St. Ignatius mission.

"Judge" Jasper Rand was a lawyer. From here he went to Livingston where he worked up a large practice. There he died.

C.C. Ralls was an "old wood workman," to quote Judge Woody. He made chairs and lived near Stevensville.

Isaac Carruthers kept a roadhouse at Clinton, known as "Dirty Ike's Place."

Baptiste Ethier was a miner and rancher. From Frenchtown he moved to the reservation.

J. W. Wells came from Salt Lake. He was a freighter.

Joseph Blodgett, a Salt Lake Mormon, died on the Flathead reservation.

E. W. Parks had a ferry at the mouth of the St. Regis river. He sold out and went to Washington.

C. Lavasseur was a merchant at Hell gate.

N. Fitzstubbs was in charge of the Hudson Bay company's post on the other side of St. Ignatius. He went to Nelson, B.C.

Dr. J. B. Busker came from California to Idaho and then here. He served as probate judge and died here.

December 1911

ABORIGINAL HORSE TRADERS

There are a good many of the things which we count as our resources which the Indians overlooked during the ages long period when they were the unchallenged lords of this vast, rich northwest. There were many of the endowments of this region which they disregarded entirely, but the rich blue-joint grass of these western Montana valleys was not one of them. The Indians well knew the value of the forage which grows here now and which grew here then. Their cattle were sleekest, their horses were strongest and fleetest. The stock which was raised by the Selish tribes was in demand by all the tribes. Those who were strong enough came over and stole the horses they wanted; those who were not able to steal, traded when they could. But the horses of the western Montana valleys were the best horses known in the northwest, even before the white man came and improved their breeding.

The Flatheads in the Bitter Root valley were rich in horses. So were their cousins, the Pend d'Oreilles of the Mission valley, and their other relatives, the Nez Perces, whose home was on the west side of the Bitter Root mountains in the rich meadows of the Coeur d 'Alene and the Clearwater. The earliest white men to enter this region found great herds of fine horses in these valleys. Some of the Indians were owners of thousands. It was not always the chiefs who were richest in horseflesh. The leadership of the Selish tribes was not bartered. It was usually a hereditary honor and the positions of war chiefs were determined by personal valor. The acquisition of these herds by some of the members of the western tribes appears to indicate that there are Rockefellers in every race and Morgans among every people, who attain fortunes at the expense of their fellows, whether wealth be measured by the standard of dollars, of horses or of clam-shells.

Some of these wealthy Indians, perhaps, secured their fortunes by trading. Others, unquestionably, gave some attention to the breeding of their stock. But the great fortunes in Indian horseflesh were made by gambling, for the Indians were always willing to bet themselves naked on the result of a horse race and many a herd has been doubled through the winning of a contest of this sort. In an earlier trail story I have told of the heavy wagers made upon a race between Indian women on the "Course du Femmes," near Arlee. Then there were raids in which the Flatheads were the aggressors and which increased the size of their herds through acquisitions from the Crows and the Blackfeet. There were get-rich-quick plans among the aborigines no less bold than those of today and certainly not as questionable.

The richest of the Indians of this region were the Nez Perces. The same reason which had prevented their decimation in warfare protected their herds from the east-side raiders— the geography of the situation was such as to make it almost impossible for the Blackfeet to reach the Nez Perces when they came west for war or robbery or for both; the lands of the Selish lay close to the west slopes of the main divide, while the Nez Perces were further protected by the high wall of the Bitter Root range. The Flatheads in the Bitter Root valley had fine herds and some specially good individual animals. The Upper Pend d 'Oreilles, whose range was between Missoula and Flathead lake, had also some excellent animals. Each tribe was proud of its herds, though the ownership was private, and each would back to the limit the racers of its braves. Next to the winning of a battle, the tribal instinct was strongest in a contest on the racecourse. Sometimes, it is true, warfare developed in a contest on the racetrack. But, as a rule, the Indians were good losers — they were real sports.

With the coming of the whites, the Indians found added opportunity for trading in horses and, later, when the real immigration set in and the travelers to the north-Pacific coast passed through this region and the country to the south, they began to acquire cattle in addition to their original horses. The stock which the immigrants drove or led often became footsore and unable to travel and the Indian picked up many good bargains in this way. They were shrewd traders and he was a mighty fortunate immigrant who got the better of them on a horse trade or any other deal.

When Governor Stevens left Lieutenant Mullan in the Bitter Root valley to survey a possible over land road through this mountain region, he left with him a considerable band of horses. Later, when Lieutenant Mullan began the construction of the famous trail which bears his name, he had large herds of stock which he recuperated and wintered in the Bitter Root and its neighboring valleys. Baron O'Keeffe and his brother David came to this valley and had their attention directed to its fertility through having charge of one of Mullan's winter herds. From these herds the Indian stock men succeeded in getting some good blood to breed with that of their own animals. They were ever alert to grab a bargain.

"Nobody ever traded quickly with an Indian," said Judge Woody to me the other day, "and this was specially true when they were bartering for horses. They traded deliberately and with solemnity as if they were debating questions of state. A horse-trade was carried through with all the formality of a council. There were two or three pipes smoked over every horse that was swapped and there was any amount of parley with each pipe smoked. The Flatheads had a great many buckskins; these were tough horses and were in demand. When they bought up a bunch of horses for trade or for sale, they always showed the poorest one first. They would haggle over the price to be paid for this animal until they had forced it up as high as they thought they could get it. Then they would close the deal and would bring in a horse that was a little better than the first. The start in the negotiations would be made at the figure received for the poorer animal and would be boosted as high as the patience of the white man would stand. This concluded, there would be a better horse trotted out. This performance would be repeated as long as the Indians had any horses left. The Indian usually got the price he wanted. Time was no object to him and the white man was usually in a hurry.

"The Nez Perces had, as I have said, the largest herds of the Indians of this region. Five Crows, one of the Nez Perce chiefs, had four thousand horses. Reuben, another Nez Perce who was locally famous, had nearly six thousand in his herds. In these herds, the finest horses were big, rangy roans. There were some exceptionally fine animals in these bands. The roans came from some horses that were brought from the coast by the Nez Perces, obtained by trade and otherwise from the Umatillas and other tribes on the salt water, who had secured them in their southern raids, getting them from the Mexican and Spanish stock men in California. There was better size to these animals than to some of the others and the Nez Perce herds were the envy of their neighbors.

"These big herds were handled upon practically the same system which was later adopted by the white stock men of the ranges," said Judge Woody when I asked him about some of the details of the old Indian horse business. "They were cut up into small bands and assigned to different ranges. The owners had riders who looked after the separated bands in a general sort of way. The roundup was an Indian feature, too. Occasionally, the entire holdings of a big Indian would be assembled. I suppose this was as often for the purpose of making a demonstration as for the need of finding out how many there were.

"The introduction of the better-bred horses came, as I have said, through the acquisition of foot sore stock from the immigrants who could not afford to spend on the trail the time which was necessary for the recuperation of the trail-worn animals. The Indians and the white traders would take these foot-sore animals and turn them into the meadows in western Montana and in a few weeks the hoofs would grow out and the stock would be fat and as good as ever. In this way some really fine stock was brought into the country.

In this way, also, the Indians obtained cattle. Draught oxen and milch cows wore out on the long tramp over the plains. Some of the Hudson Bay company's men saw the possibilities which lay in this situation and entered into the trading business for themselves in preference to continuing with the company. Neil MacArthur, who was well known in western Montana and Idaho, was one of these. He became a successful stockman and freighter through his enterprise in this direction. Fort Hall in Idaho was a favorite trading point. It was on the old Oregon trail and there the travelers usually rested after their journey across the plains and before entering upon the trip through the mountains. Here many good animals were picked up and sent into the Bitter Root valley.

It seems strange, but it is vouched for as a fact by old timers, that the Indians were exceedingly fond of milk and when they began to acquire cows as a part of their stockholdings, they reveled in the luxury. The squaws, of course, had to do the milking. They had their own method for performing this operation, as they had for doing everything else which they undertook.

"When a squaw went to milk," said Judge Woody, continuing his description, "she wouldn't touch a cow until the hind legs of the animal were tied. This, of course, was to prevent the cow from kicking and it might have been necessary at first. But when the cows got used to the squaws and the latter got used to the cows there was nothing to indicate that it was anything more than a habit. The tying was a mere formality. The bit of rope would be loosely thrown around the hind legs of the cow and the creature would stand as quietly as if she were hog -tied."

It is easy to imagine the early experiences which led to this practice of tying the hind legs of the cows. It is not a stretch of the imagination to picture a squaw picking herself up from a wreck of bucket and a plaster of milk and mud and conversing in gutturals very earnestly with that cow.

Anybody who has lived on a farm knows how mean a cow can be when she gets the kicking habit. I have heard from early farmers in western Montana some amusing stories of experiences with cows which had been purchased from Indians. The animals would never- no matter how quiet they were — submit to being milked unless they were at least given the impression that they were tied.

"We had a cow on the farm when I was a small boy," said A. J. Violette when I asked him the other day what he knew about Indian milking, "that my father had bought of an Indian. She was as gentle as could be in every other respect, but she would not be milked unless she thought she was tied as to her hind legs. All that was necessary was just to toss a little piece of rope around her hind legs. That gave her the idea that she was tied fast and she would stand stock -still as long as that rope was there. But if anybody ever tried to milk her without the rope, she would kick the milker on the top of the head every time.

"The Indians, as far as I can learn, didn't cut hay for the winterfeed for their stock. They relied entirely, as did the eastern-range stockmen later, upon the grass which cured standing. But the early white stockmen, of whom MacArthur was a type, naturally thought it necessary to prepare some hay to carry them through the winter. They guarded their meadows and saved them for the winter feed. And it was splendid forage which they found in these valleys of western Montana; it required but a short experience to prove to them that there was no better grass anywhere and it was to the Bitter Root and its neighboring valleys that the early stockmen brought their horses and cattle whenever they could.

"The first job I had in Montana," said Judge Woody, while we were talking about this subject, "was cutting hay. When we drove our ox teams down the Bitter Root valley on that first trip I ever made here, Bill Madison and I were asked by the man who was in charge of the MacArthur stock near what is now Corvallis, if we wanted a job cutting hay. We told him

164

we did but we had to go through to Hell Gate with our outfit. As soon as we had completed our contract with the freighter and had delivered our ox -teams at the Hell Gate river, we went back up the valley. It was October, but the frost had not touched the grass more than to nip the tops a little in places. I never saw a finer stand of grass than that was. The meadow where we did the cutting was, I think, a part of the McLeod ranch now. It was waist–high in fine grass and we went at it with hand scythes. Then we cocked it up with forks, eastern fashion, before getting it stowed away. There was a big lot of cattle ranging near there and they were fat and playful. They didn't seem to care much for our hay, but they delighted in tossing our little stacks about. We would have the work to do all over. Several nights they repeated this performance. They would go at the haycocks with their horns and toss the hay about faster than a machine would do it now. They made us a lot of extra work, but we were working by the day and we had been so long following oxen on the trail that the work didn't seem irksome. Anything would have been a good change from whacking steers on the trail."

Along the Bitter Root, in the valley at the mouth of the Coriacan defile, in the Frenchtown meadows and on the flat near where Superior now stands— in each of these places, the early stockmen wintered their stock. These localities were early selected as the best in the country. On the other side of the Bitter Root divide, the great stretches of bottomland along the Coeur d 'Alene furnished another favorite field. How excellent was the judgment of these pioneers in the stock business, later experience has shown. They have since become the sites of the finest farms in the world— these same valleys. There has been some of the finest stock ever grown developed upon these fields; there are some of the best orchards on earth growing now upon the slopes above those meadows.

We who have seen the peerless Ogden, the matchless Hamburg, the gallant Tammany go forth from the pastures of the Bitter Root to wonderful victories on the eastern turf; we who have watched the prowess of Prodigal, Red Cherry, Brown Silk, China Silk and Doctor Spelman after they left their paddocks in, the Bitter Root valley; we who have gloried in the triumphs of the Bitter Root colors on eastern tracks— we know of the later conquests of the stock which was nurtured upon the forage of these western Montana fields.

We who have seen the cattle go from these valleys to the great markets of the world and there command, year after year, the highest price paid for beef; we who have seen the butter record of the world challenged by the Mills Jersey herd, sent out from its Lolo home in the lower Bitter Root- we know what magic there is in the forage which grows upon the meadows of this great valley.

We are proud of the record that has been made by western Montana stock and we are inclined to think that we have made a great discovery in finding out the wonderful properties of the grass which grows here. We have a right to boast of the superiority of our hay and our grain- each merits the highest honors. But we have found nothing new. The Indians knew as much as we of the properties of Bitter Root grass, long before a white man had ever set foot upon this valley.

The fame of the horses which were raised in the Bitter Root in the Indian days was great – comparatively as great as the reputation of the stock which is sent out from there now. The horses of the Flatheads were as fine as any that were known. We have intensified the application of the forage which grows upon our fields;

we conserve it and we improve its quality as we are able; but we have only retained it in the position which it occupied under Indian dominion. It was the best in the world then. It is only that now. We have developed other resources amazingly; we have unearthed some of which the Indian never dreamed; we have found use for others which he spurned as of no value; but we are no wiser than he in our application of the grass of our meadows. The aboriginal stockman was keen - it seems to be a way with stockmen to be keen. He knew it took good grass to produce good stock and he found where the good grass was. We have followed the trails he blazed, we have walked in the paths which he trod in many directions. But in none have we followed more precisely in his footsteps than in our development of the stock –raising industry. The modern horse trader is cited as the type of shrewdness which is sharp to the extent of disregarding the strict truth; but the Indian horse trader of a generation or two ago was his counterpart; the modern could give no pointers to the ancient; the white could add nothing to the shrewdness of the red.

There is some of the old Indian stock left. In some parts of the reservation, the old Indian ponies are yet to be found. But most of the red men have improved their stock. There are some mighty fine animals now in the red man 's herd. In this respect he has kept up with the times. He has taken more kindly to stock raising than to any other branch of agriculture for it is the heritage of the Flathead and the Pend d 'Oreille and the Nez Perce to love good horses and to do anything he can to get them. His forefathers had the best horses of their time. He aspires to the same distinction. There will not be any Indians at all, one of these days, but the last Indian will have the best horse he can get. It may not be a very good horse, for that last Indian is apt to be a specimen of hard luck, but it will be the best horse he can get and if he has a chance to trade it for a better one, he will do it. Don't think, however, that he will trade it for a poorer one. He will not, because he is an Indian and because it is a horse.

Following Old Trails by Arthur L. Stone
January 1912

Note:

Rather condescending essay in regard to indigenous people of western Montana. If you can overlook the condescension, this in an interesting piece showing us how early white settlers and native peoples interacted in the old west.

WALDRON A PIONEER OF MONTANA

Man Who Met His Death In Alaska was an Early-Day Freighter in this State

"Dave Waldron was a good, reliable, A1 man. I knew him well in the early days, and so did everybody in the western Montana camps. Everybody liked him. I am sorry to hear that he is dead, and I am grieved to know that his death was so painful." This was Judge Woody's comment yesterday after he had read in the Missoulian's dispatches of the death from fire of David Waldron, northwest pioneer, who perished in Alaska.

"In western Montana, in the years from sixty-two to sixty-four, I knew Waldron well," continued the judge. "He ran a little freight outfit between Walla Walla and the camps here. He came to Hell Gate, Deer Lodge, Bannock and Virginia City. His outfit consisted of two or three packhorses and a riding horse. He used to bring us the Sacramento Union, the Alta Californian and the Oregonian. We paid him a dollar a copy for these newspapers, and we were glad to get them. Going back he would take a list of names and would inquire at Walla Walla for letters for us. If he brought us letters we paid him a dollar apiece for them, and were devilish glad to get them, even at that price.

"I see the press dispatches say he was once on the vigilante committee, and that he also served as a sheriff in Montana. I do not think that is so. He may have been a sheriff later, down in Washington, but I am sure he was not in office at all in Montana. He was known as 'Dave' Waldron in every camp this side of Virginia City. We used to watch for him with anxiety; He made the round trip about once a month, and was very regular. He came in over the Coeur d'Alene trail or around by Lake Pend d'Oreille, according to the season and the stage of the water. He kept up his trips until 1864, when Montana mail began to come in by way of Salt Lake. Then he went down to the coast and discontinued the service.

"Years ago I heard of him in Los Angeles, where I was told he made a lot of money. I have not heard of him since until this morning, when I read in The Missoulian of his painful death up in Valdez. I wonder what took him into Alaska. It must have been the call of the wilderness. He belonged to the frontier; he was out of place anywhere else, not because he was rough, but because he was naturally attached to the wilderness."

"He was a kindly, gentle man. He did many favors for us when he furnished us the only means we had of communicating with the outside world. He was all right---an A1 man."

November 1912

WHEN FISHING WAS EASY

Annual Banquet of Angler's Club of Missoula

"When Fishing Was Easy," was the subject assigned to Judge Woody, who was introduced as the oldest fisherman in Montana. Judge Woody told about the days when he first came to Montana and the Missoula river was still as clear as the Bitter Root, or any other streams of Montana. He talked about the great big red-bellies which were thick in the rivers at that time and described the old-style fishing as compared with that introduced by Judge Bickford and others from the east, who came in here with their tenderfoot method of fishing with automatic reels and bamboo poles.

"Why," said the judge, "it took the fish three of four years to get used to their new-fangled ways. We just took a horsehair line, caught some grasshoppers, cut a willow pole when we got to a likely-looking place, made a couple of casts and we had a fish. It didn't take us over half an hour to get all we could carry home. In those days we didn't play with a fish. We yanked him out of by main strength and awkwardness. Those were the days when the fishing was good and there is no joke about that. The only thing that makes me sad as I talk about the old times tonight is that my comrades of those days have all passed over to the other shore and I am the only one that is left. It wasn't scientific fishing in those days, but we brought home the fish and didn't have to run in and exhibit proudly after we hunted up a pair of scales and found that it weighed half a pound. There were no placer miners muddying the streams and it was the best fishing in the world."

October 1912

Notes:

The red-bellies Judge Woody was referring to were probably Westslope Cutthroat Trout. As he mentioned, mining severely reduced the fish population in many Montana rivers. The institution of the EPA and the emphasis on cleaning the air and water in western Montana has led to a resurgence in the fish population.

This meeting would have occurred during the time of Reverend Maclean (from *A River Runs Through It*) in Missoula. One has to wonder if he or his sons were members of the Angler's Club.

In the Interest of Political Equality

Parlor meetings will be held Friday and Saturday afternoons in the interest of political equality, under the auspices of the Equal Suffrage league of the university. One for the Third ward will be held at 3:30 o'clock Friday afternoon at the home of Judge Woody on West Pine street. Miss Jeanette Rankin, Miss Mary Stewart and Judge Woody will address the meeting. At 4:30 o'clock a meeting for the First ward will be held at the home of Mrs. John Rankin on Madison street. Miss Jeanette Rankin, Miss Stewart and Miss Stella Duncan will speak. At 7:30 in the evening, Miss Zerr, Miss Rankin and Miss Stewart will address a meeting at the home of Mrs. Tylar B. Thompson on East Front street. The speakers and hours of the meetings for Saturday will be announced later. All persons who may be interested in the campaign for equal suffrage in Montana are urged to attend at least one of these Meetings.

October 1912

Notes:

Judge Woody's daughter, Alice, was involved in many progressive causes which her father supported. It is likely that she asked him to host and speak at the meeting. Women got the right to vote in the United States in 1920, eight years after this meeting.

Jeanette Rankin was the first woman elected to serve in the U.S. Congress, representing Montana. She is the only representative who voted against the U.S. fighting in World War I and World War II.

THIS WAS IN THE EARLY DAYS

––––––

Stories Suggested by Judge Woody's Address

––––––

CAMELS ON THE LO-LO TRAIL

––––––

When the Mules Saw the Importations From the Eastern Deserts They Broke for the Timber and Howled Like Mad

The very interesting address of Judge Woody before the board of trade last evening has recalled many interesting incidents regarding early times in Missoula. Judge Woody mentioned briefly the pack train of camels that was brought in here to carry freight from Walla Walla to Missoula and points up the Big Blackfoot. The animals were a part of the band that the government imported for freighting across the Mojave desert. They could carry heavier loads than a mule train, but were so much slower that they did not meet with the expectations of the men who introduced them and were not used very long. There are many stories told of the experiences of these camels in the Mountains. They were in charge of a Turk with an unpronounceable name which nobody remembers, and the mountain trails proved too much for them. The Turk was in constant trouble with other packers, as his camels were a constant terror to mules and horses and their appearance would throw an ordinary pack train into consternation.

One incident is related of a packer who was returning to the coast with a long mule train and up on the divide near Saltese met the Turk and his camels. The sight of the first camel and as one after another of the strange beasts appeared the mules quit squarely and broke for the timber. It was a perfect stampede and the packers were delayed for a week in rounding up the frightened mules. The poor Turk was blamed for it all and tried in vain to appease the wrath of the mule-skinners. They had it in for him and his camels and the poor Moslem never came so near to getting a thrashing and then missing it.

But probably the most ludicrous incident that occurred while the camels were in use here was one which Eph Hackett told to a STANDARD reporter to-day, and which is familiar to all old timers. The camel train was somewhere in the upper Blackfoot country, when a fierce storm overtook them and the animals were driven into a quaking asp grove for shelter. There they huddled, their tawney sides being dimly visible through the quivering leaves of the thicket, while the storm raged around them. A party of prospectors was at this time crossing the valley, and one of them, an Irishman, caught sight of the camels as they stood in the brush. He thought they were moose and saw an opportunity to win fame as a hunter. Motioning to his companions in a cautionary way, he whispered, "Kape schtill, byes, and we'll get them, ivery wan." No sooner had he said this than he drew a bead on one of the poor creatures and it fell dead where it stood.

Then the poor Turk was wild. He tore his hair and called upon Allah and the prophet to be his witness that the infidel dogs were after him. He called down upon the poor Irishman all the curses in the extensive vocabulary of a Mohammedan and prayed vehemently that the Irishman's seed might wither upon the face of the earth and his name be forgotten. He was finally appeased by the payment of several hundred dollars, and the Irishman never won fame as a hunter of moose.

This unpopularity of the camels and the fact that the mountain trails were so difficult, caused the camel train business to lapse into innocuous desuetude in a short time and the Turk and his train returned to a climate where there is warmer weather and less water than there is in Montana. But they are distinctly remembered by all of the old-timers, who tell stories by the yard of the days when camels brought supplies into Missoula.

The other story that was suggested by Judge Woody's address is the account of how "Wildcat Bill," the original settler of Missoula, started a monte game and skinned everybody and how the suckers got their money back. Bill was running the game in his cabin and had won about all the dust that there was in the camp. One day his victims got desperate and determined to get even with the fellow in some way, so they called a quiet meeting and laid their plans. Bill went into the hills a short time after this and, while he was absent, his victims pulled out the staple in his cabin door and gained entrance to the room where they had dropped their dust. They found the cards and marked them. Then when Bill came back they went against his game again. This time they were uniformly successful and they didn't stop playing until Bill had lost more than he had won from them. The fellow never knew how they beat him and kept playing. In the hope of finding out. But his fondness for money was greater than his curiosity and he finally quit. But his victims would have played until the cards wore out.

February 1885

Note:

The camel story seems to grow more elaborate with each re-telling.

A NOTABLE ANNIVERSARY

December 10 is a date notable in the history of Missoula. It is the anniversary of the founding of a home which has been for the last 42 years a haven of hospitality and a fine inspiring influence. Last Wednesday, December 10, marked the 80th birthday of Judge Franklin Hargraves Woody and the 42nd anniversary of his wedding with Miss Sarah Elizabeth Countryman, which was solemnized in Missoula at the home of Horace Countryman.

Both bride and groom are beloved by old-time friends and by those of later years. Both are actively interested in the social and civic welfare of Missoula and of Montana. Both are gently touched with the marks of long years of service rendered. After being most insistently urged by a reporter for the Missoulian, Mrs. Woody consented to tell the following story of her wedding to be read by those who like to know the life story of pioneers who laid the foundations of this city.

The Story

"Rev. William H. Stoy, a presbyter of the Protestant Episcopal church residing at Deer Lodge, came to the little village of Missoula especially to perform our wedding ceremony. The stage brought him through deep snow and intense cold on Saturday, the day before the wedding.

"The home of Horace Countryman was a small wooden structure standing on the corner where the Elks' temple now stands. There a few intimate friends

179

assembled to witness the marriage ceremony at 6:30 o'clock in the evening. Those of the company still living, so far as I know, are Mrs. Lizzie Kennedy, Mrs. Emma Dickinson, Mr. Billy Edwards of Seattle and Mr. and Mrs. T. R. Dana of Sheridan, Wyo., Jacob Reinhard and Henry Meyers. The wedding cake was made by Mrs. F. L. Worden and Mrs. T. R. Dana. The bride's gown was made by a "Worth" who chanced to be in Deer Lodge for a short time and the remarkable feature of the dress was its big pocket, something uncomfortably lacking in gowns of today. Mr. Woody had sent east for his wedding garments and there was much uneasiness on account of a delay in their arrival. They came, however, on the same stage with the officiating clergyman, and there was great rejoicing. The ring did not come in time and one that had belonged to my mother took its place. There was an hour of wedding feast and congratulations, then we all went to the courthouse to attend divine service held there by Rev. Mr. Stoy. The trip of a few blocks was made with difficulties even in a cutter. The snow was so deep and so drifted that the old family horse could hardly flounder through. From the sleigh to the door of the courthouse, Mr. Woody took 'all his worldly goods' in his arms and carried her through the snow. Shortly after our return from the church service we were greeted and treated to a charivari, whole-souled and well meant. In those days a charivari was more sincerely a compliment than it is at the present time.

"In retrospect, I see 42 years rich with joy and interspersed with sorrows; 42 years of 'for better or for worse.' Do young people when taking the solemn vows dream of the meaning of those words? We are so glad of the few old friends who are left to hark back with us through the memories of those precious 42 years, and we are so thankful for the younger new friends who have come into our circle. We thank our heavenly Father for His loving kindness to us, that we continue to be together."

ELIZABETH COUNTRYMAN WOODY
December 1913

Note:

Emma Dickinson was the first schoolteacher in Missoula.

Elizabeth ("Lizzy") Woody opened the first Sunday School in Missoula and was one of the town's first teachers.

FIRST MONTANA CITIZEN DIES AT MISSOULA HOME

Last Sunday's Missoulian gives the following account of the death of Judge Frank H. Woody, reputed to be the oldest pioneer citizen of the state of Montana at the time of his death:

Judge Frank H. Woody, "first citizen of Montana" and this city's first mayor, died shortly after noon yesterday at his Missoula home, 328 West Pine street. Death came quietly to the aged pioneer, following an illness so brief that Mrs. Woody and a daughter Flo Woody Anderson, had not time to reach Missoula from California, whence they were summoned at the first sign of danger. Frank H. Woody, Jr., and Miss Alice Woody, the two other children, were with their father when he died.

Judge Woody had been a resident of Montana longer than any man now living. And since his coming in October, 1856, he has constantly been a leader in the state. He was one of Missoula county's first clerks; was the first mayor of Missoula; served for many years as judge of the Fourth judicial district; was first editor of the Missoulian. He was elected too, to one of the state's earliest legislative assemblies, that of 1869, though he did not serve. In his later years he was an active and able practitioner of law and, naturally, prominent in the Society of Montana Pioneers.

Judge Woody came to Montana in August, 1856, and was 83 years old at the time of his death. Funeral services were held Monday under the auspices of the Masonic and Odd Fellows lodges of Missoula.

December 22nd, 1916

Was In State Before Any Man Now Living

Passing of Judge Frank Woody of Missoula, Recalls Historic Times; In Same State Was Resident of Four Territories

A few days ago there died in Missoula at the age of 83, Judge Frank H. Woody, who came to Montana before any man now living. He entered the borders of what is now Montana in 1856, driving a team of oxen, and when he arrived at the site of Missoula, he found an encampment of 300 Indian lodges where the city was to rise. He became the first mayor of Missoula, and from 1866 to 1880 served as county clerk and recorder, which, in the later years, was combined with the post of probate judge. In 1869 he was elected a member of the territorial legislature for the counties of Missoula and Deer Lodge, but as there was doubt of the legality of the session that followed he did not attend. He lived for 50 years in the same house in Missoula, which was situated consecutively in the territory of Washington, the territory of Idaho, the territory of Montana and eventually in the state of Montana. As a matter of fact, he informs us in a memorandum he left that he really lived in four territories and one state, while yet within the boundaries of Montana.

"When I first came to what is now Montana," he wrote, "and lived in Grass valley, within eight miles of what is now the city of Missoula, the country was then Washington territory. I then went to Bannack, in 1862, at that time in the territory of Dacotah; then in 1864, I came back to Hell Gate, five miles below the present city of Missoula, which was in the Idaho territory; then it became Montana territory and then the state of Montana."

December 29th, 1916

LAWYERS HONOR WOODY

Members of Profession Revere Name of First
Judge of District

The following resolution was adopted by the bar
association of the fourth judicial district yesterday in
honor of Judge Frank H. Woody, who died December
16, 1916. The resolution was drawn by a committee
consisting of Judge John E. Patterson and W. L. Murphy,
appointed at a special meeting of the association the day
after Judge Woody's death:

"On the 16th day of December, 1916, Frank H.
Woody passed from mortal life. On that day an
unusually long and uncommonly active career was
suddenly concluded, not after the gradual weakening of
a robust body, nor following the long breaking down of
a strong and virile mind, but rather like the slowing and
stoppage of an engine when fuel is no longer fed into its
fires.

"The amazing physical strength and endurance
possessed by Judge Woody, his ability to withstand the
rigorous ordeals of pioneering; to resist the attacks of
disease and even forestall for so long the assaults of time
itself, was only commensurate with and equal to the
wonderful vitality and strength of mind, which kept his
mental faculties clear and active to the last hour of his
eighty-three years.

"In this community where Judge Woody lived for
nearly sixty years, he took no more of the attributes of an

institution than of an individual. Upon the scroll of his wonderfully retentive memory was written every phase and incident of the development of Western Montana; every fact and factor which has entered into the upbuilding of this city and its vicinity, from the earliest beginnings of civilization here until the last hour of his life, have passed, in orderly succession before his eyes and found a permanent record in his memory.

"The loss to local history in original sources of information caused by Judge Woody's death is not possible of calculation, but it can be truthfully said that with him died the accurate record of many facts of highest historical value, which during his life, he never found time to commit to writing. One of the great benefactors of this commonwealth has passed away.

"His service to Montana was not of that spectacular kind which leaves behind great industries and work of tangible construction requiring the outlay of large amounts of capital, but rather in that essential and necessary service which paved the way for these later developments. Born in the state of North Carolina at a time when the hardiest of the veterans of the Revolution were yet among the living; when the stories of New Orleans and Lundy's Lane were being recounted by actual participants therein, he early turned his face toward the setting sun and took up the battles of peace and civilization against the forces of barrenness and savagery in the rough wilderness of the Rocky mountain tablelands. He came to western Montana for a temporary sojourn in the fall of 1856, and took up his permanent residence in this valley in 1860, and lived here continuously thereafter for fifty-six years. Thus at the time of his death he was a Montana Pioneer of Pioneers, the sole historian and eye witness of the drama in which the missionary priests and the French voyagers were the only white actors. His eye glanced farther back into the dim beginnings of Montana civilization than that of any other man. His indomitable will and tireless hand played the chief part in laying the foundation stones of Montana's splendid growth and development and the commonwealth and its inhabitants must ever remain his grateful debtor.

"It is not the legal profession alone that feels the loss of this sturdy oak, but in view of the fact he was for long the venerable dean of active practitioners within this judicial district; that he strove valiantly, as judge and counsel to clarify the law, to uphold the standard of legal ethics and to enhance the repute of our profession among the people, be it

"Resolved, By the members of the Fourth Judicial District Bar association, in which resolution the faculty and students of the law school of the State University of Montana join, that while the legal profession has lost a mighty soldier in the cause of right and justice and the state of Montana has been deprived of the living presence of him whose life typifies the highest development and best traditions of good citizenship, yet we are grateful that an all wise Providence has vouchsafed to such a character years beyond the allotted span of life in which to round out and complete a noble career; and, be it further

"Resolved, That while we are duly thankful for the privilege of association for so many years with one whose life and character have been an inspiration to the members of the legal profession and an uplifting influence to all citizens, yet we feel most keenly the sorrow of the final parting and extend our deepest sympathy and condolence to the devoted wife and children whose grief we share and in whose just pride in the accomplishments of a distinguished husband and father we claim a part."

January 1917

The following essay is Judge Woody's very thorough treatise about the early history of western Montana and Missoula written for the Montana Historical Society in 1877. It is mostly a rehash of stories you've already read earlier in this book but there are some new stories and much detailed historical information. He was quite proud of this work and referred to it often throughout the years.

A SKETCH

OF THE EARLY HISTORY OF
WESTERN MONTANA
BY
JUDGE F. H. WOODY

———

All that portion of Montana Territory bounded on the North by the British Possessions, on the East by the main range of the Rocky Mountains, on the South and Southwest by the Bitter Root Mountains, and on the West by the one hundred and sixteenth degree of longitude, and embraced within the limits of Missoula and Deer Lodge counties, at one time constituted a portion of the vast domain of the great Northwest known as Oregon Territory. When, and by what means, the Government of the United States obtained title and possession of the great Territory of Oregon, are facts not generally known. Oregon was for a long number of years claimed by both the United States and Great Britain, and was held in joint occupation by citizens of both nations. Great Britain claimed by the right of discovery, and the United States by the right of discovery and by virtue of the French cession of the territory of Louisiana, of April 30, 1803, and the treaty of limits with Spain, of February 22, 1829, and also by right of actual occupation of the soil for a long number of years. The "Oregon Question" engrossed the attention of Congress for a number of years, and came near in resulting in a war between the United States and Great Britain, but the matter was amicably adjusted by the treaty of June 15, 1846 by which the forty-ninth parallel of latitude was established as a boundary line between the two nations and the United States became the sole and undisputed owner of all that portion of Oregon lying South of that line.

Oregon was organized as a Territory by act of Congress, passed Aug. 1818, and included within its limits, all that portion of Montana lying on the west side of the Rocky Mountains.

By an act of Congress approved March 2, 1853, the Territory of Oregon was divided, and this portion of it became a portion of Washington Territory. The first legislature of Washington Territory created the county of Clarke, named in honor of Captain Clarke, of the Lewis and Clarke expedition. Clarke county extended from a point on the Columbia river below Fort Vancouver, to the summit of the Rocky Mountains a distance of some six hundred miles. This portion of the present Territory of Montana, was then a portion of Clark county, and was for the first time included within the limits of a county.

Clarke county was afterwards divided, and the county of Skamania created, and we became a portion of Walla Walla county, with our county seat located on the land claim of Lloyd Brooks on the Walla Walla river, in the present Territory of Washington.

Walla Walla county was afterwards divided and we became a part of Spokane county, with the county seat located at Fort Colville.

We remained a part of Spokane county until December 14, 1860, when the Legislature of Washington Territory, divided the county of Spokane, and created the county of Missoula, with the county seat at or near the trading post of Worden & Co., Hell's Gate Ronde.

The county of Missoula, as first established, embraced all those portions of the present counties of Missoula and Deer Lodge, lying on the West side of the main range of the Rocky Mountains. Missoula county remained a portion of Washington Territory, until Idaho Territory was organized, on the 3rd day of March, 1863, when it became a portion of that territory.

The first legislature of Idaho created Missoula county with nearly the same boundaries that it has at the present time, and located the county seat at Wordensville. On the 26th day of May, 1864, Congress created Montana Territory and the first Legislature, which met at Bannack, created on the 2nd day of February, 1865, the county of Missoula and located the county seat at Hell's Gate. From the foregoing it will be seen that Missoula county has at different times compromised a portion of four Territories and five counties.

Probably the first white men who visited this portion of Montana, were Lewis and Clarke, who with their party, sometime during the summer of 1805, entered the Bitter Root valley from the south, through a pass known at the present time, as the Big Hole Mountains, near the head of the Bitter Root river. It was in Ross' Hole, a small round valley near the head of the Bitter Root river, where the party of Lewis and Clarke first met and gave the name of Flatheads to the tribe of Indians now known by that name.

A number of years since, the writer was well acquainted with Moise, the second chief of the Flatheads, who was a boy at the time when Lewis and Clarke passed through the Bitter Root valley, and well remembered the event and many circumstances connected therewith, the party being the first white men ever seen by these Indians. Moise was a warm and devoted friend of the whites from the time of his first meeting with them, up to the time of his death, which occurred about ten years since.

191

Western Montana has been occupied from time immemorial by three different Indian tribes, to-wit: The SALISH---called by Lewis and Clarke Flatheads, and by which name they are generally know---The Kelespelnins, now exclusively known by the French name of Pen d'Oreilles, and the Kootenais. These tribes speak dialects slightly different, and most probably constituted at a remote date, one tribe or nation. They have a tradition that they came from the far North but this tradition is exceedingly vague and indefinite.

From the time of Lewis and Clarke's expedition up to about the year 1835 or '36, we have no definite knowledge of what transpired in this portion of our present Territory. At a very early date a number of Canadian voyagers and Iroquois Indians from Canada, visited this country, and sometime between 1820 and 1835, the employees of the Hudson's Bay Company visited it for the purpose of trading with the Indians and extending the power and dominion of that gigantic company, but these early adventures left us no available data from which to write their travels and adventures.

About the year 1835 or 36' the Flathead Indians, who inhabited the Bitter Root valley, had gathered some little knowledge of the Christian religion from the Canadian voyageurs and Iroquois Indians who visited the country for the purposes of trapping and trading for furs. The Flatheads were anxious to gain further knowledge, and sent to St. Louis, Mo., for a priest, or as they called him, a "Black Gown." Three different parties of Indians were sent in as many different years. Of the first party sent but little that is definite is known, except that none reached St. Louis. The second party on their downward trip were all killed by Indians---probably Blackfeet, ---near Ft. Hall. The third party started in the spring of 1839, and some time in the summer of that year two of the party reached St. Louis. Of the two who successfully accomplished the journey, one was named Ignace Iroquois and he died at or near the St. Ignatius Mission in Missoula county, sometime during the winter of 1875-6.

The other was the father of a Flathead named Franscois Saxa, of Bitter Root valley. The Superior of the Jesuit establishment at St. Louis promised to send them a priest in the following spring. Ignace remained in St. Louis all winter and came up with the father in the spring. The other Indian came back the same fall to tell the news. In the spring of 1840 Father De Smet and Ignace came across the plains and found a camp of Flatheads and Nez Perces near the Three Tetons, near the eastern line of the present Territory of Idaho. The Father baptized a few Indians, and came with the Flatheads to the Gallatin valley, near the place where Gallatin City now stands, and finding that he could do but little without aid, returned to St. Louis for assistance. In the spring of 1841 Father De Smet returned, coming by way of Fort Hall. He brought with him two other Fathers---Point and Mengarine, and several Lay Brother, among whom were Brothers W. Classens and Joseph Specht, now residing at St. Ignatius Mission, and who are eminently entitled to the appellation of "oldest inhabitants," having been residents here for more than the third of a century. The party brought with them wagons and carts, horses, mules and oxen, and came by way of the Deer Lodge valley and down the Hell's Gate canyon. These were the first wagons and oxen brought to Montana. In the fall of that year the first settlement was made in the Bitter Root valley, by the establishment of St. Mary's Mission on the tract of land upon which Fort Owen is now situated. During the fall and winter of the same year, dwelling houses, shops and a chapel were built and nearly all of the Flatheads and some Nez Perces and Pen d'Oreilles were baptized.

Probably the first farming attempted in our Territory was in the spring of 1842 by the fathers at the Mission. This year they raised their first crop of wheat and potatoes. The same year the first cows were brought from the Hudson's Bay Company's post at Fort Colville, on the Columbia river. About this time or a little later, the Fathers also erected saw and grist mills--- the burs for the latter being brought from Belgium.

In 1844 the Coeur d'Alene Mission was established by Fathers Point and Hoecken.

After establishing the St. Mary's Mission, Father De Smet returned to St. Louis, and thence went to Europe, but returned to the Bitter Root valley in 1844, making his third trip, and bringing with him a number or Fathers and Lay brothers: among the number was the well known and highly esteemed Father Ravalli, late a resident of this county.

St. Mary's Mission was kept up until November 1850, when the improvements were sold by Father Joset to Major John Owen. The bill of sale---now in possession of the writer---bears date, St. Mary's Mission, Flathead Country, November 5th, 1850, and is without doubt, the first written conveyance ever executed within the limits of Montana.

The St. Mary's Mission was abandoned for the reason that the missionaries were continually harassed by the numerous war parties of Blackfeet that visited the valley on their marauding expeditions. These war parties were so numerous and murderous that no man's life was safe away from shelter. In 1849, while Father Ravalli was in charge of the mission, having with him one Lay Brother and a few Indians, the Mission was attacked by a war party of about fifty Blackfeet, that proceeded to make it quite uncomfortable for the Father and his companions. During the attack two bands of horses belonging to the Mission and Flathead Indians made their appearance, and the Blackfeet preferring horses to scalps, withdrew from the attack, drove off the horses and left the occupants of the Mission to meditate on their narrow escape.

After the abandonment of St. Mary's Mission, the Fathers and Lay Brothers were sent to the different missions that had been established further northwest.

St. Ignatius Mission, situated on the present Flathead reservation, was established by Father Hoecken in 1851.

In 1847 the Hudson's Bay Company established a trading post on Crow Creek, on the northern portion of the present Flathead reservation, and the place is still known as the Hudson's Bay Post. Angus McDonald, Esq., who came to the mountains as early as 1838 or 1839, and who is now a resident of this county, was probably the first officer placed in charge of the new post.

In 1849 Major Owen started from St. Joe, Mo., as sutler for a regiment of United States troops known as the Mounted Rifles, destined to for Oregon. The troops came as far as Snake river, when winter caught them, and they built winter quarters on the bank of that river about six miles above Fort Hall, where they spent the winter. The camp was called Cantonment Loring and the place was long known by that name. Major Owen remained at Cantonment Loring until the troops resumed their march in the spring of 1850, when he relinquished his sutlership, and spent the summer on the emigrant road, trading with the emigrants bound for California and Oregon. In the fall of 1850 he came to the Bitter Root valley, and having bought the improvements of the Catholic Fathers, erected a trading post at that point and christened it Fort Owen, a name which it still continues to bear at the present time. The fort was constructed of a stockade of logs placed in an upright position with one end planted in the ground. The stockade was necessary to protect the inmates and their property from the incursions of the numerous war parties of the Blackfeet Indians, that continued to make raids into the valley up to 1855. It was the custom to drive the horses inside of the stockade each night during the spring, summer and fall of each year, to prevent them from being stolen by the Blackfeet; and even this precaution did not always save them. One night a party of Blackfeet came to the fort, and with knives and sticks dug up some of the logs forming the stockade, and drove away all of the horses belonging to the fort.

In the fall of 1852, while hauling hay, a young man named John F. Dobson, from Buffalo Grove, Illinois, was killed and scalped by the Blackfeet in sight of the fort. The writer of this, has in his possession a diary kept by Dodson from the day that he left Illinois in the spring 1852, up to the day he was killed. The last entry that he made in it, was on the day before he was killed, and is as follows: "Sept. 14th, 1852, I have been fixing ox yokes and hay rigging. Helped haul one load of hay. Weather fair." The next entry is in the hand writing of Maj. Owen---apparently made the next day, and in these words: "Sept. 15th. The poor fellow was killed and scalped by the Blackfeet in sight of the Fort." These facts are only cited to show with what trials, dangers and privations the early settlers of Missoula county had to contend.

After Maj. Owen purchased the property since known as Fort Owen, he made many improvements. He enclosed land and commenced farming---rebuilt the grist and saw mills, and in after years, tore down the old stockade of logs, and built a large and substantial fort of Adobies or sun dried bricks. He opened and kept a regular trading establishment supplying the wants of both whites and Indians. The stock of goods and supplies were kept up by making a trip each summer to The Dalles in Oregon, with pack horses, usually going down in the spring by Clark's Fork and the Pen d'Oreille Lake, and returning during the latter part of the summer by an Indian trail over the Coeur d'Alene Mountain.

Fort Owen was the nucleus around which the early settlers gathered, obtained supplies and sought protection in the hour of danger. It was known far and wide for the hospitality that its generous proprietor extended to the early settlers and adventurers in this distant---and at that time---almost unknown wilderness. Major Owen on his annual visits to Oregon, and from other sources, had accumulated an excellent library of several hundred volumes, which he kept open for the use of his friends, and being one of the most genial and companionable of men, it is not surprising, that Fort Owen was a favorite resort for the early settlers and hardy mountaineers—or that the Major is oft and kindly remembered by those who have reason to remember his kindness. Times have wonderfully changed since the days of which we write. Major John Owen has left Montana to spend his remaining days amidst the scenes of his boyhood, and Fort Owen, that contains a history within itself, has passed into the hands of strangers and is fast falling into decay, and in a few more years will be numbered amongst the things of the past.

Sometime about 1849 or '50 a number of trappers and hunters, who for a number of years had followed trapping and hunting in the mountains relinquished in a great measure their former occupation, and turned their attention to trading with the immense immigration that annually thronged the great overland thoroughfare from our western frontier to California and Oregon. Among the number were Joseph Lompre, William Rodgers, Ben and Jim Simons, Ben Keiser, Gabriel Prudhomme and others. These men led a regular nomadic life. Spending the summer on the emigrant road, they would trade for large numbers of poor and sore footed cattle which they would drive to some good wintering place on Green river, or to the Beaver Head or Bitter Root valleys and the "Road" as it was usually termed, which continued for many years, and by which means many of the Flathead Indians became possessed of large herds of fine cattle.

This emigrant trade brought a number of persons into the valley to engage in trade with the Indians, among whom were Thomas W. Harris, now of the Bitter Root valley, and C. E. Irvine of Deer Lodge, who came here about 1851 or '52.

Somewhere between 1850 or '54, an old Mexican trapper by the name of Emanuel Martin, but generally known as "Old Emanuel," brought wagons into the Bitter Root valley from Fort Hall or Salt Lake. These wagons were brought through the Big Hole Prairie, and over the Big Hole Mountain and down the Bitter Root river. Old Emanuel spent a lifetime in the mountains and knew the country perfectly from Mexico to the British Possessions. He died near Fort Owen some three years since.

In March 1853, the Territory of Washington was organized, and Isaac I. Stevens appointed Governor of the same. He was also interested with an expedition fitted out from St. Paul, Minnesota, to make the first survey to determine the practicability of a route for a Northern Pacific Railroad. This expedition arrived in what is now Missoula county, in the fall of 1853, bringing with it a number of men who afterwards became citizens of Montana, among whom were Capt. C.P. Higgins of Missoula, and Thomas Adams and F. H. Burr who were for a long time residents of Missoula and Deer Lodge counties.

In the fall of 1853, Lieut. John Mullan, a member of the expedition, was directed to establish winter quarters in the Bitter Root valley, and to make certain observations and explorations during the winter. His party consisted of a few soldiers and citizens, among the latter were Messrs. Adams and Burr. Lieut. Mullan erected four buildings of logs at a large spring at the mouth of Willow creek, in the Bitter Root valley, and named the place Cantonment Stevens, in honor of the commander of the expedition.

At this time (1853) Fort Owen with a few cabins built near by Indians and half breeds, and Cantonment Stevens comprised all of the buildings in the Bitter Root valley.

In the fall of 1855, Neil MacArthur, an old Hudson's Bay trader, having retired from the company's service, came to the Bitter Root valley accompanied by L.R. Maillet and Henry Brooks. McArthur brought with him a band of horses and cattle and located and occupied the buildings at Cantonment Stevens, and engaged in stock raising. Governor Stevens having, during the summer of 1855, concluded a treaty with the Flatheads, Blackfeet, Crows and other mountain tribes of Indians, the Blackfeet had in great measure eased making raids into the Bitter Root valley, and lives and property were comparatively safe.

The treaty between the United States and the Confederated Flathead nation, consisting of the Flatheads, Pen d'Oreille and Kootenai tribe, was

199

concluded in a council held in July 1855, in a large pine grove on the river about eight miles below the present town of Missoula, and opposite to the farm of John S. Caldwell. The place was for a number of years known as Council Grove.

In 1854, the first white woman came to the country now constituting Missoula county, and was probably the first white woman who honored our Territory with her presence. In that year a Mrs. J. Brown came from the East, and while crossing the Rocky Mountains gave birth to a male child, now grown to manhood and a citizen of a neighboring Territory. She, with her baby and two little girls, rode alternately a stout hardy Manitoban steer and a Canadian pony. She visited the Hudson's Bay Post in the northern part of our county and remained several days, and proceeded the same season to her present residence in Washington Territory. This was probably the first white child born within the limits of our present Territory, but as we do not know at what point Mrs. Brown crossed the mountain, we cannot assert it as a fact.

In 1854, Gov. Stevens appointed Thomas Adams Special Agent for the Flathead Indians. In 1855, the Government appointed the first regular Agent for them in the person of Dr. Landsale of Oregon. The Dr. established his agency at the mouth of the Jocko river, and erected one or two log cabins but made no permanent improvements. The Agency remained at this place until 1860, when it was established at its present location by Maj. John Owen, who had succeeded Lansdale as Agent. In the spring of 1856, Dr. Lansdale went to Ft. Hall, and while there engaged Henry G. Miller and his wife Minnie, to take charge of the Jocko Agency: Miller and his wife arrived here the same spring, and remained at the mouth of the Jocko till the fall of 1857, and then went to Walla Walla. This was the second white woman who visited our county, and the first one who made it her residence. Miller and his wife came here again in the fall of 1860 and remained during the following winter. They afterwards returned to Utah Territory and settled permanently. Mr. Miller died a few years since, and Mrs. Miller is still residing in the latter Territory.

Just here it is proper that some explanation should be given as to some of our local names and their derivation. The Bitter Root valley and river are so called from a root that grows abundantly in that valley, and which is largely used by the Indians as an article of food. The root has a strong bitter taste, and is anything but palatable to a person unaccustomed to its use. The early Catholic Fathers called the valley and river, St. Mary's, and by that name it appears on some of our older maps. The large round valley lying below and adjacent to the present town of Missoula was called by the early Canadian trappers who visited this country, "Hell's Gate Ronde." And the river, "Hell's Gate river." The name Hell's Gate originated in this wise: In an early day when the war-like Blackfeet overran the whole of Montana, the romantic and picturesque pass or canyon where the Hell's Gate river cuts through the mountain above the town of Missoula, was a regular rendezvous for their war parties, and so constantly did they infest this place, that it was almost certain death for an individual or even small parties to enter this pass, and so great was the dread and fear entertained by the Indians of the Western tribes and the Canadian voyageurs, in their language, port d'enfer, Gate of Hell, or Hell's Gate, and from which the river , and subsequently a village took their names. The writer has never been able to find a translation for Missoula. The word appears to have been first used and applied by Lieut. John Mullan: as to where he obtained it, or what it means, we are left in doubt.

In the fall of 1856, several parties who had been spending the summer trading on the "Road," relinquished that business and came to the Bitter Root valley and took up their residences, among whom were T.W. Harris, Joseph Lompre and Wm. Rodgers. An unusually large number of Indian traders also came to the valley that fall. In October of that year the following named parties came into the valley: Van Etten, a Mormon trader, with three ox teams and with him George Goodwin, James Brown, Bill Madison and the writer hereof, Hooper & Williams outfit, consisting of one mule and two ox teams, and with them, George and Frank Knowlton, brothers-in-law to the Hon. W. H. Hooper, of Utah, Arch and Alma Williams, brothers of Thos. Williams, of the firm of Hooper & Williams----- Merrill and Portugee Louis. There also at the same time Robert Hereford, who at a much later date was county assessor of Lewis and Clarke county. All of these parties with their wagons and teams came in at the head of the Bitter Root valley. Upon our arrival in the valley we found Henry Brooks and Thos. Adams at Cantonment Stevens, and at Fort Owen, Henri M. Chase and wife, W. W. Tallman and Louis Robonin, commonly called Louis Marango. The last named parties had been driven out of the Nez Perces' country by the Indian war of 1855-56, Major John Owen, P. M. Lafontaine and Delaware Jim, at that time being absent on a trip to Fort Benton with ox teams. These parties, with the Fathers and Lay Brothers at the St. Ignatius Mission, constituted the entire white population of the country now known as Missoula county. In November of the same year Fred H. Burr came in from Salt Lake by the same route, bringing three wagons and a large band of cattle, and with him came Judge C.E. Irvine, now of Deer Lodge, George Hatterbaugh, John Saunders, called "Long John," and John Silverthorne, now of the Bitter Root valley; and still later in the season came Neil McArthur with three ox teams, and with him L. R. Maillett, James Holt, ----- Jackson and an odd specimen of humanity named Bill West, but commonly called "Pork" for short. If time and space permitted, the reader could be regaled with many reminiscences and narrations in which "Pork" played an active part, and the ludicrous was a prominent feature.

I will, however, relate one of "Pork's" adventures in which he played the role of doctor in a manner that was ludicrous enough at the time, but which resulted fatally to his patient, and had the facts been known to the Indians at the time, would have caused serious trouble to the few whites then in the country. The facts are these: During the winter of 1856-7 "Pork" Jackson, Madison, Holt and the writer were employed by Neil McArthur and were encamped in Council Grove, in what is now known as Grass valley, and about nine miles below the present town of Missoula. A number of lodges of Pen d'Oreille Indians were encamped near us. Sometime during the winter, an Indian boy about twelve years old, grew sick, and the matter coming to the knowledge of "Pork," he proposed to doctor him, as McArthur had a large medicine-chest in camp, containing various kinds of medicines, but he was advised not to do so, as he was ignorant of the nature and use of medicines---being unable to read or write---and he might kill the Indian and involve us in trouble.

He would not take our advice, but insisted that he knew what he was doing, that he had often given medicine to Mary and the children back in southern Missouri. He overhauled the medicine chest and finding some pills administered some of them to the Indian boy who gradually grew worse, and the Indians, not having a very high opinion of "Pork's" medical skills, sent over to St. Ignatius Mission for one of the Fathers who came over, and after examining the boy, pronounced it a case of pneumonia, and leaving the boy some medicine, returned to the Mission. The boy improved for a few days and was in a fair way to get well when "Pork" again took him in hand. In rummaging through the medicine chest he discovered a vial or small bottle without any label and containing a dark colored liquid which he pronounced sweet wine, and proposed to give some of it to the boy, as he said it was just the thing that he needed to give him strength. He was advised to let it alone, but he insisted that he knew what he was doing, and do it he would. He filled a small vial with the medicine and directed a squaw to give the boy a teaspoonful of it three times each day, and the result was that on the next day there was a dead Indian in camp. The Indians did not mistrust anything and nothing was said about the matter for some weeks, except when some of the boys would joke "Pork" on his success as an Indian doctor. A few weeks after the death of the Indian we had occasion to move our camp a short distance, and while moving the medicine chest, the stopple came out of one of the bottles and some of the contents of it were spilt on "Pork," and actually burnt a hole the size of a man's hand in a pair of new buckskin pants. A few days after this "Pork" left for California. One day, a short time after "Pork" had left, Holt said to me that he believed "Pork" killed the Indian boy, and upon being asked for his reason, he said that the medicine that had spoiled "Pork's" pants was the same bottle out of which he had given the Indian the sweet wine. Upon examination of the bottle it was found to contain some

204

powerful kind of acid, and was beyond a doubt the cause of the Indian boy's death. Had the Indians known it, "Pork" would have paid dearly for his experiment, and when we found out the actual fact is the case, we were careful to keep them to ourselves, and the Indians know nothing of the matter up to the present time.

Van Etten wintered in the Jocko: McArthur stopped at the Cantonment: Burr built houses on the west side of the river near the mouth of what is now known as Fred Burr creek: George Knowlton, in charge of Hooper & Williams' teams, located on Grant creek, just above the farm now owned by Abner G. England, and the creek for some years afterward was known as Knowlton's creek. About the first of December, Frank B. Owen, David Pattee, and one or two other men arrived from Ft. Colville, and later in the month Maj. Owen and P. M. Lafontaine returned from Benton, bringing the first goods over that road with ox teams. During the winter of 1856-7, the population of the Bitter Root valley was larger than it again was until the fall of 1860. Up to this time no settlement had been made in the Hell's Gate Ronde. Soon after the arrival of Mr. Pattee, he contracted with Maj. Owen, and commenced the erection of a grist and saw mill at Fort Owen. In the latter part of December, 1856, McArthur having determined upon erecting a trading post in the Hell's Gate Ronde, dispatched Jackson, Holt, Madison, "Pork" and the writer to Council Grove to get out the necessary timbers to erect the buildings the next summer. Our quarters consisted of an Indian lodge and we fared sumptuously on bread and beef, with coffee without sugar about once a week. The snow fell deep during that winter, and the weather was quite cold, but we lost but little time and by spring had gotten out a large quantity of square timber. In the spring McArthur paid

205

us off for our winters' work, each man receiving a Cayuse horse in full of all demands. With the coming of spring there was a general breaking up of winter quarters and not many men were left in the country. Burr drove his cattle to the "Road," going by way of Deer Lodge, and with him went "Pork," Jackson, Madison, "Long John," Hatterbaugh and some others whose names are forgotten. A party of two or three went to Benton and went down the river, among whom was F. B. Owen. Van Etten and Knowlton with the respective parties returned to Salt Lake with large bands of horses. Adams and Hereford went to the "Road" to trade. McArthur and Brooks moved their stock to Hell's Gate Ronde---or as it was commonly called Hell's Gate---and located on the land now owned by J. S. Caldwell. James Holt and the writer still remaining in the employ of McArthur, broke about eight acres of land and sowed to wheat and also planted a garden. This was the first attempt made at farming in the Hell's Gate Ronde. The potatoes, carrots, beets, turnips and onions grew well, but the wheat, while in the milk, was completely killed by a heavy frost on the night of the 14th of August, 1857. McArthur was absent during the entire summer and fall, having gone to Colville and thence to the Suswap mines in British Columbia. In those days we did not have our daily papers and telegraphic dispatches containing the latest news from all parts of the globe, but considered ourselves fortunate if we got one or two weekly Oregon papers in six months; Eastern papers we never saw. The following will show our isolated condition; The Presidential election was held in November, 1856, but we knew nothing of the result until about the middle of April, 1857, when Abram Finley arrived from Olympia, with a Government Express for the Indian Department, bringing two or three Oregon papers from which we learned that Buchanan had been elected and inaugurated President.

During the summer of 1857, Jas. M. Minesinger, now of the county, came to the Bitter Root valley, having come to the Beaver Head valley the previous fall with John Powell. In the fall of this year, Hugh O'Neil and a man named Ramsey, came to Hell's Gate from the Colville mines, on the Columbia river, and were employed by Mr. Brooks to put up two buildings with the timber cut the previous winter. These were the first houses put up in Hell's Gate Ronde. But few events of historical interest occurred from the fall of 1857 to the fall of 1859. During the spring and summer of 1858 an Indian war in the Spokane and lower Nez Perces country cut off communication with the West, and placed the settlers of this county in a dangerous situation. Congress having made a large appropriation to build a Military Wagon Road from Fort Walla Walla to Fort Benton, placed Lieut. John Mullan in charge of the work. He organized his expedition at the Dalles, Oregon, in the spring of 1858, but was forced to disband it on account of the Indian hostilities. He again organized in the spring of 1859, and constructed the road over the Coeur d'Alene mountains as far as Cantonment Jordan on the St. Regis Borgia, where he went into winter quarters, sending his stock to the Bitter Root valley. During the winter the greater portion of the heavy grades between Frenchtown and the mouth of Cedar creek was constructed. In the spring of 1860, he resumed his march and took expedition through to Fort Benton, doing but little work however, between Hell's Gate and Fort Benton.

In 1858 or 59, Baptiste Ducharme and Louis Brown, two old mountain men, located farms and built houses, where they now reside near Frenchtown,

Ducharme came from French Prairie, Oregon, and Brown from Colville valley. About 1859, R. A. Pelkey and W. Bills located farms and built houses in the Hell's Gate Ronde, in what is now known as Grass Valley. About the same time Angus McLeod and James McIver settled on "Two creeks." Also about the same time, Capt. Richard Grant, a former officer of the Hudson's Bay Co., and for many years a well known trader on the emigrant road, came to the Bitter Root valley, and resided there during the winter, and in the spring of 1860 removed to Hell's Gate, and resided during the summer about two and a half miles below the present town of Missoula, and in the fall of that year, built houses and settled on the creek that now bears his name some four miles north of the town of Missoula. Capt. Grant was the father of Mrs. C.P. Higgins, of Missoula. He, with his eldest daughter died at Walla Walla in the spring of 1862, while on a visit to that place. His widow, Mrs. Helen Grant resided at Hell's Gate until her death in 1863. In the spring of 1860, Maj. John Owen, having been appointed Indian Agent to succeed Dr. Lansdale, abandoned the old agency at the mouth of the Jocko, and established it at its present site. A large number of men were employed, a farm opened, buildings erected and saw and grist mills built, putting in circulation a large amount of money and making times lively generally.

In June, 1860, Frank L. Worden and C. P. Higgins, under the firm name of Worden & Co., started from Walla Walla with a stock of general merchandise for the purpose of trading at the Indian agency, but upon their arrival at Hell's Gate, they determined to locate at that point, and accordingly built a small log house and opened business.

This was the first building erected at that place and formed the nucleus of a small village that was known far and wide as Hell's Gate, and which in later years, had the reputation of being one of the roughest places in Montana. The town originally stood upon the tract of land now owned by Clices Lavasseur. During this year 400 United States troops under the command of Major Blake passed over the Mullan road from Fort Benton to Fort Walla Walla and Colville. During the fall of this year a number of settlers came into the county, and new farms were taken up at Frenchtown, Hell's Gate and in the Bitter Root valley, and during the winter of 1860-1, a considerable number of men wintered in the different settlements.

On the 14th day of December, 1860, the bill creating Missoula county was passed by the Legislative Assembly of Washington Territory. The county extended from the 115th degree of longitude, east to the summit of the Rocky Mountains, and from the 46th degree to the 49th degree of latitude, which included all that portion of Deer Lodge county lying west of the Rocky Mountains. The bill creating the county appointed the following named persons offices:

C. P. Higgins –	County Commissioner
F.L. Worden –	County Commissioner
T. W. Harris -	County commissioner
M. W. Tipton -	Sheriff
H. M. Chase -	Justice of the Peace

Of the above named officers none of them qualified except C. P. Higgins and Thos. W. Harris, and the only business that they did was to advertise an election in 1861 and canvass the votes.

The county was attached to Spokane county for judicial and Legislative purposes: and we were allowed one representative with Spokane. The first election held in Missoula county was a general election in June or July. Polls were opened at Fort Owen, Jocko Agency and Hell's Gate and the entire vote polled was seventy-four (74.) Wallace, Garfield and Lander were candidates for Congress, and lander received the entire seventy-four votes. Dr. Bates, of Spokane county, was elected representative. The following county ticket was elected:

Henry Cloren -   Probate Judge
John Beadle -   Treasurer
Wm. T. Hamilton -   Sheriff
Frank H. Woody -   Auditor
Granville Stuart - County Commissioner
C. P. Higgins -   County Commissioner
H. Van Dorn -   County Commissioner
Henry Brooks -   Justice of the Peace

None of the officers qualified except the county commissioners, auditor and justice of the peace, and as there was no business to transact, no records were kept. The commissioners met once or twice but had no business, no bills to audit nor assessment rolls to correct. The only business for county commissioners and their clerks in those days was to meet annually to canvass the votes of the different precincts and serve their constituents without reward.

In the spring of 1861 Lieut. Mullan organized another party and started for Fort Benton to finish up the road that he had merely opened the year before. His expedition was accompanied by an escort of one hundred men under command of Lieut. Marsh. The expedition came as far as the crossing of the Big Blackfoot river, where they erected winter quarters and named them Cantonment Wright, in honor of Colonel, afterwards Gen. Wright, who quelled the Indian war of 1858 so effectively. During that winter the heavy grades in Hell's Gate canyon were constructed. In the fall of

1861, R. A. Pelkey and wife, G. A. Pelkey, wife and child, Mrs. Mineinger and child, Mrs. Queen Pelkey and Wm. Tisson arrived from St. Louis, Mo., and settled at Hell's Gate. The same fall Peter J. Bolte opened a saloon at Hell's Gate, being the first one opened in the country.

The winter of 1861-2 was one of the most severe ever known in the mountains. Prior to this time stock raisers had never made any preparations to feed their stock, consequently no feed had been put up. The weather was extremely cold and the snow fell deep. In February, 1862, a thaw came, and while the snow was soft it turned cold and the snow was frozen perfectly solid, rendering it impossible for stock to move or get feed, and the result was that hundreds of cattle died, as did many horses.

The expedition of Lieut. Mullan and the building of the Jocko agency brought a large number of men to this county, and a number of them remained and are now prominent citizens of our county, among whom are, W. B. S. Higgins, John S. Caldwell, C. C. and D. C. O'Keeffe, E. D. Dukes, John Chatfield, Charles Shaft, and some others whose names the writer had forgotten.

On the 5th day of March, 1862, the first marriage of two white persons in Missoula county was solemnized at Hell's Gate; that of George P. White to Mrs. Josephine Mineinger. The ceremony was performed by Henry Brooks, Justice of the Peace, and who was ever afterwards known as "Bishop Brooks." This was probably the first marriage of white persons within the limits of the country now Montana. On the 13th day of February, 1862, at Grass valley, near Hell's Gate, there were born to R. A. and Adeline Pelkey, a son, who was christened Jefferson Henry Pelkey, and is now residing at Walla Walla. This was the first white child born in Missoula county, of which we have authentic information.

The first lawsuit ever commenced in Missoula county, or in fact in Montana, was commenced and tried at Hell's Gate, in the month of March, 1862, before Henry Brooks, Justice of the Peace. The proceedings were under the laws of Washington Territory. A Frenchman called "Tin Cup Joe"---other name forgotten---accused Baron O'Keefe with beating one of his horses with a fork handle and then pushing him into a hole thereby causing his death, and claimed damages in the sum of forty dollars, and sued O'Keefe to recover that amount. The place of trial was in Bolte's saloon. A jury of six was empaneled and sworn to try the case. W. B. S. Higgins and A. S. Blake, now of Missoula county, and Bart Henderson, of the Yellowstone, were of the jury. As the trial progressed the proceedings became less harmonious until it ultimately culminated in a bit of unpleasantness between the defendant and the writer, who was acting as attorney for the plaintiff. During the unpleasantness the friends of the respective parties lent a hand, and it was far from being a select or private affair. While the unpleasantness was in progress, the Court and a portion of the jury had fled for dear life, and when harmony was restored, they were no where to be found. After considerable search the Court and jury were captured and the trial proceeded.

The case was finally given to the jury, and after a brief absence they came into court and rendered a verdict for plaintiff for $40 damages. The costs swelled the judgment to about $90. This was probably the most hotly contested case ever tried in the Territory. The defendant endeavored to take an appeal to the District Court, but as that court was held in Colville, three hundred miles distant, he concluded to settle the

212

judgment, which he did. Poor Bishop Brooks was, in 1865, killed in Uncle Ben's Gulch, near Blackfoot City, shot through a glass door by whom or for what cause was never known.

In the fall of 1861, A. S. Blake came here with the intention of prospecting, and in the spring of 1862 in company with "Bud" McAdow, W. B. S. Higgins, Dr. Atkinson, C. P. Higgins and E. D. Dukes went to Gold Creek and commenced operations, where a number of the party engaged in mining during the summer of 1862.

In the spring of this year Cantonment Wright was broken up. Mullan with his party going to Benton and the escort under Lieut. Marsh returning to Walla Walla and Colville. During the summer of this year Henry W. Miller and family came from Colorado, and settled near Frenchtown, being the first white family in that settlement. During the summer another election was held under the laws of Washington Territory, and polls were opened at Hell's Gate, Jocko Agency, Fort Owen and Gold Creek, and L. L. Blake elected a member of the Legislature, but never attended. At the same election James Stuart was elected sheriff of Missoula county.

On the 3rd of March, 1863, Idaho Territory was organized and this county became a part of that Territory and an election was held in the fall of that year for members of the Legislature. The writer has no knowledge that any county officers were appointed by the governor of Idaho for this county, and from the fact that Montana was organized on the 26th of May, 1864, he is of the opinion that none were appointed.

In 1863, when the country was overrun with road agents and horse thieves, Missoula county received her full quota of them, Plummer and Rives making their appearance at Hell's Gate as early as August, 1862.

In January, 1864, the vigilance committee of Alder Gulch sent a party of the committee to Hell's Gate to arrest and hang certain parties supposed to be in this county. The party arrived at Hell's Gate about the 23rd or 24th of January.

Skinner, one of the men for whom they were looking was keeping a saloon at that place, and this was the headquarters of the road agents. Here the vigilantes found and hung Cyrus Skinner, Alick Carter and Johnny Cooper. The same night they caught Bob Zachary and George Shears. Shears was hung on the farm now owned by J. R. Latimer.

Skinner, Cooper, Carter and Zachary were all hung upon the same pole placed over the top of a corral at Hell's Gate. Bill Graves---called "Whisky Bill" ---was the next day caught and hung near Fort Owen.

In April, 1864, the citizens of Hell's Gate suppressed in a summary way what threatened to be a serious Indian outbreak. In the fall of 1863, a young Pen d'Oreille Indian killed a man named Ward, in the Hell's Gate canyon, near the place where Baker's station is now located. In the spring of 1864, this same Indian having been joined by a number of young bucks bid defiance to, and threatened the lives of several of the white settlers, and even fired at one Frenchman. The citizens sent a courier to Deer Lodge and Alder gulch for assistance. John Powell and one and two others came from Deer Lodge, and a few men from Alder gulch, but before the latter arrived, the Indians became alarmed, delivered up the guilty Indian when the citizens very deliberately hung him upon the same pole upon which the Road agents were hung a few months before and this ended the trouble. This was the kind of peace policy believed in by our early settlers.

The Kootenai mines having been discovered early in the spring of this year, hundreds of men flocked to them, passing by the village of Hell's Gate. This stampede created a demand for all kinds of supplies and everything sold at war prices. In the spring of this year, seed wheat sold as $10.00, and potatoes at $6.00 per bushel; yeast powders were cheap at $1.50 per box and coffee at $1.00 per pound, and flour of the poorest quality sold readily at $30.00 per hundred pounds and everything else in proportion. In the fall of 1864, the ruling price for wheat was from four to six dollars per bushel. The currency at this time was principally gold dust. These high prices were caused by the immense number of people who had flocked to the mines of Alder and other gulches on the East side, and by the demand made by the settlers in the Gallatin, Jefferson and Madison valley for seed grain and potatoes. In the fall of this year, under the proclamation of Governor Sidney Edgerton, an election was held for delegate to Congress and members of the Legislature. Frank L. Worden was elected member of the Council, and John Owen, Representative, but when the legislature convened, Owen did not attend, and E. B. Johnson was admitted to the seat. In November of this year, Matt Craft killed a man named Crow, at Hell's Gate. In February, 1865, James Doran killed two men, named ------- McLaughlin and Wm. G. Cooke, at the same place. The fight was between Doran and McLaughlin, and Cooke was probably shot accidentally. About January 1, 1865, a man named Watson was found murdered in a house near Fort Owen. A man named Fogarty was arrested and charged with the murder and after having an examination before Thomas Roup, Justice of the peace, was held to answer on a charge of murder , and placed in charge of a special officer to convey him to Bannack

215

City, but when the officer arrived at Fort Owen, the citizens took charge of the prisoner, and being with him, they hung him at the Fort Owen mill. The first officers under the Montana organization were appointed as follows:

Geo. P. White -   Probate Judge
Charles Shafft -   County Clerk
A J. Campbell -   Sheriff
Charles Shafft -   Justice of the Peace
Thomas Roup -   Justice of the Peace

On the 4th of September, 1865, a regular election was held and the following county officers elected:

E.S. Miller -   Probate Judge
Henry W. Miller - County Commissioner
C. C. O'Keeffe -   County Commissioner
Fred Loveland -   County Commissioner
Henry P. Larrabie - Sheriff
Charles Shafft -   County Clerk
David Pattee -   County Treasurer
E. A. P. Hillman -   Superintendent of Public Instruction
George P. White - Coroner

Under the above named officers the county was first regularly organized on the 16th day of October, 1865. On this day the first account was presented and allowed against Missoula county.

During the winter of 1864-5, Worden & Co. erected a saw mill at the place where Missoula now stands, and in the spring of 1865 commenced the erection of a grist mill and business house, and in the fall of the year moved their store from Hell's Gate to their new building. Other buildings were put up by other parties, and thus was the town of, Missoula established, and was at first called Missoula Mills, but eventually the last part of the name was dropped by common consent.

The town of Frenchtown was established in 1864, Stevensville the same year and Corvallis about 1868. In December, 1865, Tom Haggerty shot and killed Matt Craft in the town of Missoula. It was a cold blooded and cowardly murder, but as Craft was a bad and dangerous man and a terror to the whole community, but few were sorry to hear of his death. In the spring of 1866 J. P. Shockley committed suicide at Hell's Gate, and was the last victim who died a violent death at that place. In February, 1866, the board of county commissioners, upon their responsibility, moved the county seat from Hell's Gate to Missoula, where it was subsequently established by the Legislature. In this year the first assessment of property was made and the first taxes collected.

In the spring and summer of 1865, rich and extensive gold mines were found on Little Blackfoot river and its tributaries, and also on the tributaries of the Big Blackfoot river, in Deer Lodge county, that induced an immense immigration from California and Oregon, and from the Territories of Idaho and Washington. Nearly all of the vast crowd of gold seekers came over the Coeur d'Alene mountains by way of the military wagon road constructed by Lieut. John Mullan, and passed through the Hell's Gate Ronde. During the whole of the summer and the fall of 1865, the road was literally lined with men and animals on their way to the new El Dorado. At this time a large portion of the supplies used in the mining camps of Montana, were purchased in San Francisco, Cal., and Portland, Oregon, and were transported from Walla Walla, Washington Territory, on pack mules, over the Coeur d'Alene mountains, by way of Hell's Gate and Missoula to the various mining camps of Montana. So great was this trade, that hundreds and even thousands of pack mules were employed in this business, and times were unusually lively in Western Montana. It was during the summer of 1865, that some parties brought up by this same route from Nevada or Idaho, a number of camels loaded with merchandise. These were the first, and I believe the only camels ever brought to Montana, and were a source of wonder and surprise to the Indians, who had never before seen anything like them. The adventure did not prove a success to the parties engaged in it. One of the camels died at the Mullan crossing of the Missoula river below Missoula, another one was shot and killed near Blackfoot City, by a hunter, who had never seen a camel, and who thought it was a moose. The same lot of camels are now doing duty in Arizona, packing merchandise from Yuma City to the interior.

It being impossible to cross the Coeur d'Alene mountains earlier than the month of July, the spring travel came up by the Pen d'Oreille Lake and the Clark's Fork of the Columbia. The vast amount of travel over this route each spring, together with the expectation that the Northern Pacific Railroad would speedily be completed and would undoubtedly pass down Clark's Fork, induced the Oregon Steam Navigation Company of Portland, Oregon, to put a line of steamboats on the lake and river for the purpose of shortening the land transportation to Montana. The company commenced operations in the fall of 1865, and in four months from the time the first tree was felled for her, a steamboat was launched and floated on the bosom of the lake. She was 108 feet in length, 20 feet beam and was 85 tons burden and constructed entirely of whip-sawed lumber. This boat was built on the western shore of the lake in Idaho Territory. She was christened the Mary Moody, and made her first trip in the spring of 1866, coming across the lake and up Clark's Fork, about fifteen miles to the

Cabinet Landing, just inside of Montana. This was the first steamboat that ever navigated the waters of western Montana. The following winter the company constructed two more boats to ply on Clark's Fork above the Cabinet mountains. One of these, the Cabinet, ran from the upper edge of the Cabinet falls, to the rapids at Rock Island; and the other one, the Missoula, ran from the upper end of the Rock Island rapids up to Thompson's Falls. These boats did a good business for two or three years, but after that time the travel having fallen off, the boats were, in the summer of 1870, run down over the falls, to the lower or western end of the lake, when the machinery was taken out and conveyed to the lower Columbia river. That the reader may form some idea of the vast travel through this portion of Montana from 1865 to 1870, I will state, that the year of 1869, was an unusually dull year, owing to a lack of water in the mining camps, but during that year, the Steamboat Company reported that they conveyed on their boats about four thousand animals and their packs, and that many packers passed with their trains around the northern end of the lake by a trail difficult to pass in wet seasons.

From 1863 to 1866 were the halcyon days of Missoula county: money was plentiful, produce of all kinds sold at war prices, with the demand exceeding the supply, no taxes or license to pay, and our county free from debt. During the summer of 1867, mines were discovered on Libby creek in the northwest portion of this county, which were worked by a number of men during the summer. During the month of August of that year a party of four men, prospecting on the same creek, were attacked by Kootenai Indians, and three of them killed and one badly wounded. The killed were Anthony Cavanaugh, John Moore and Wm. Allen. After killing them the Indians burned or attempted to burn their bodies. The other man, Joseph Herren, was shot in the right breast, the ball passing entirely through his body. He escaped with only the clothes he had on at the time, and in this condition lived for twenty-one days, subsisting on such berries as he could obtain. He was found by a party of prospectors and brought to Missoula, and remained until he entirely recovered. He is now, or was a short time since, in Prescott, Arizona.

September 27, 1867, the first District Court convened in Missoula county, Hon. L.P. Williston, presiding.

During the autumn of 1869, Louis A. Barrette and B. Lanthier discovered paying mines on Cedar creek, in the western part of this county. This camp drew a great many men to it, and in the spring of 1870 it contained and estimated population of 1,500 persons. The discovery of other mines in the immediate neighborhood soon followed. It is estimated by careful, competent judges that the entire product of Cedar creek and surrounding gulches, since its first discovery, has been something over $1,000,000.

According to the census of 1870, the County of Missoula contained that year, a population of 2,554 persons. Much of that population however, was transient, drawn hither by the mines on Cedar Creek. The permanent population of the county at this time--- 1877---probably does not exceed fifteen hundred and principally engaged in mining, farming, trading and stock raising.

The first newspaper published in Missoula county was issued in September, 1870, by Magee & Co., and was called The Missoula and Cedar Creek Pioneer, afterwards changed to the Weekly Missoulian, under which name it is still published.

The first churches established in Montana were established in Missoula county. The first being at the old Catholic Mission established in the Bitter Root valley, and the next that of the St. Ignatius Mission.

(What follows is a listing of various offices and the names of the men who occupied these positions. These names are of little interest to most readers, so they have been omitted. If you are interested in reading them, you can find this article on-line in its entirety.)

Historical Society of Montana 1877

Notes:

You will notice that this essay includes several stories you have already read. This is why I added it at the end of the book. It is fairly dry reading though Judge Woody did manage to include a few stories we have not seen elsewhere. For history buffs who are interested in the early days of Missoula, this is a nice resource.

Wordensville is the name they attempted to give to Hellgate Village then to Missoula. Frank Worden, a very modest man, would have none of it.

Ross' Hole is a small flat grassy valley ringed by mountains close to Sula, MT. It was named after a Hudson's Bay trader named Alexander Ross who, with a trapping brigade, was stuck there in 1834 for over a month in the winter. He spent the month attempting to break through the snow in the passes to the Big Hole Valley. Lewis and Clark visited this spot in 1805 where they encountered the Bitterroot Salish Indians for the first time. This is when they gave them the name "Flathead".

The John Mullan Military Road was built to make it easier for settlers (and troops) to move into the northwest territories. It ran from present day Fort Benton, Montana to (Fort) Walla Walla, Washington. Settlers would ride a steamboat to Fort Benton on the Missouri River then travel by wagon to their destinations in Montana, Idaho, or Washington. The route in present day is, Fort Benton to Helena then Helena to Missoula and finally Missoula to Walla Walla. Present day highways and interstates between these cities are good approximations of the path of the original John Mullan Military Road.

Bibliography

Stone, Arthur L. *Following Old Trails.* Morton John Elrod, 1913.

Woody, Frank H. *How an Early Pioneer Came to Montana and the Privations Encountered on the Journey.* Montana Historical Society Contributions, Vol. VII, pp. 138-64, 1910.

Woody, Frank H. *From Missoula to Walla Walla in 1857, on Horseback.* The Washington Historical Quarterly - University of Washington, Vol. 3, No. 4, pp. 277-286, 1912.

Woody, Frank H. *The First Fruit Trees in Missoula.* Montana Horticultural Society, pp. 30-1, 1907.

Woody, Frank H. *A Sketch of the Early History of Western Montana.* Montana Historical Society Contributions, Vol. II, pp. 88-106; 1896.

Additional Information

Bitterroot Big Hole Road/Gibbon's Pass:
https://www.fs.usda.gov/Internet/FSE_DOCUMENTS/fswdev3_009501.pdf

Newspapers

The Anaconda Standard
The Weekly Missoulian
The Daily Missoulian
The Ronan Pioneer
The Cut Bank Pioneer Press

About the Editor

Traci Rasmusson is a chiropractor in Missoula, Montana. She is also an amateur photographer and history buff. This book and her coffee table book *Finding Old Missoula* were developed during the pandemic of 2020 while she was home. Traci lives in Missoula with her husband, her sons, two cats (one nice and one cranky), a lab mix and a pug mix.

If you would like to order a copy of her coffee table book, *Finding Old Missoula*, you can buy it on the Porte de L'Enfer Publishing Facebook Page:

https://www.facebook.com/Finding-Old-Missoula-colorful-book-of-early-Missoula-history-104324138052508

https://portedelenferpubco.com/

Additional Print and E-Book Copies of *Judge Woody – History and Humor in the Old West* can be purchased at Amazon.com.

An E-Book version of *Finding Old Missoula* is also available at Amazon.com.

If you'd like to order multiple wholesale copies of either book to sell in a bookstore, contact Dr. Rasmusson at traci@hschiro.com or call (406)880-2225. Limited local pick-up of books is available in Missoula, Montana.

Books by Traci L. Rasmusson D.C.

Finding Old Missoula (2020)

Judge Woody – History and Humor in the Old West (2021)

Woody Family Photo 1896 – L to R
Beth, Flora, Lizzie, Frank Sr., Alice, Frank Jr., Franklin, Mary

MRS ELIZABETH WOODY
Grand Matron

Frank Woody Sr., Frank Woody Jr. and Horace
(son of one of Mrs. Woody's siblings)

www.ingramcontent.com/pod-product-compliance
Lightning Source LLC
LaVergne TN
LVHW041214080426
835508LV00011B/950